CONTENTS

INTRODUCTION

This book has two primary goals:

- To provide you with a sound introduction to the components, materials, and mechanics of hot water boilers that you will encounter and evaluate as a home inspector.

- To provide you with a solid understanding of inspection processes, strategies, and standards of practice that will help define the scope of your inspections. Specifically, the ASHI® (American Society of Home Inspectors) Standards of Practice are represented throughout.

The ASHI Standards are not the only standards for home inspectors, but they are widely used. Several states and other organizations have their own standards. The point is that standards help define a consistent scope of professional practice for home inspectors to use in their day-to-day work.

In its discussion of hot water boilers, this book assumes that you already are familiar with gas or oil furnaces and with background concepts of heat transfer. If you feel you need a better background in those topics, we recommend that you read the *Gas and Oil Furnaces* volume of this series first.

FEATURES OF THIS BOOK

This book is structured to help you learn and retain the key concepts of home inspection. It also will help you form a set of best practices for conducting inspections. Learning features include:

- Learning Objectives: At the beginning of each chapter you will find a list of concepts you should master by the end of the chapter.

- Chapter Review Questions: Each chapter ends with a set of review questions to help you test your understanding. Answers can be found at the end of the book so you can check your results.

- Key Terms: Important terms appear in boldface within the text discussions so you can begin to understand them in context. A summary list of key terms appears at the end of each chapter.

- Inspection Checklists: These tools summarize the important components you will be inspecting and their typical problems.

- Inspection Procedures: This material helps you develop a systematic approach and best practices for your inspections.

- Standards of Practice: ASHI has established a set of standards that are widely used to define the scope of inspection that practitioners should achieve.

- Inspection Tools: This summary list will help you build your toolkit of "must have" and optional tools for the job.

CHAPTER

1

OVERVIEW OF HOT WATER BOILERS AND HEAT EXCHANGERS

LEARNING OBJECTIVES

At the end of this chapter you should be able to:

■ list four materials used in boiler construction

■ list and describe three ways heat is moved through a hot water system

■ list ten differences between boilers and furnaces

■ list the advantages and disadvantages of hot water heat

■ list three problems found with boiler heat exchangers

1.1   HOT WATER BOILERS

The function of the boiler is the same as a furnace: to provide heat so that all parts of the home are comfortable. Boilers fulfill this function in a slightly different way than furnaces.

Boilers Don't Really Boil

Hot water boilers, or what some people call hydronic heating systems, don't really boil the water. They typically heat the water to a maximum of 200°F. Normal operating temperatures for many boilers are in the 120°F to 130°F range, depending on a number of factors, including outdoor temperature, design capacity, etc.

Steam Boilers

There are boilers that do boil water into steam. Steam boilers are not discussed in this book.

1.1.1   Materials

Cast Iron

The oldest boilers, and some modern boilers, have cast-iron heat exchangers. Cast iron, incidentally, is a very high-quality material that works very well for water heating systems.

Steel

Many boilers have steel heat exchangers. On some steel boilers, the exterior jacketing is very heavy plate steel. In other systems, the exterior jacket is light gauge sheet steel forming a cabinet that looks very much like a furnace cabinet. In either case, the exchanger steel is heavy gauge.

Steel heat exchangers are considered lower quality than cast iron, since they are more susceptible to corrosion.

Copper

Many modern boilers use copper tubes. Some have aluminum fins on the tubes, and many have cast-iron headers at either end of the copper tubes. Copper is an excellent heat transfer medium, but copper-tube boilers have a shorter life expectancy than steel and considerably less than cast iron.

Alloys

Some boilers have stainless steel or copper-nickel alloy heat exchangers. These systems are relatively new and their life expectancy and long-term performance are not yet known.

1.1.2   How Boilers Work

Several Fuels

Boilers work much like furnaces. Heat is generated by burning coal, oil, natural gas, or propane, for example. Heat can also be generated by electricity. There are electric boilers.

Distributing the Heat

Furnaces use warm air to move heat from the source to various rooms of the house. Boilers use water instead of air to move heat through the house. Furnaces have heat exchangers, and so do boilers. The fire side of the heat exchangers for furnaces and boilers are virtually identical. In a furnace, however, the distribution medium is the house air, and that's what you find on the other side of the heat exchanger. Boilers have water on the other side of the heat exchanger.

Water Is the Heat Transfer Medium

Heat is transferred from the fire side of the heat exchanger, through the heat exchanger, into the water. The water is piped to the various rooms of the house, where it is released through radiators, baseboards, or convectors (Figure 1.1).

Radiant Heating

In some homes, radiant heating is used where the distribution pipes are embedded in floors or ceilings and heat is released along the entire length of these piping grids, buried in the finishes. In radiant systems, there are no radiators or convectors. There is also a lot less for the home inspector to look at!

FIGURE 1.1 How Boilers Work

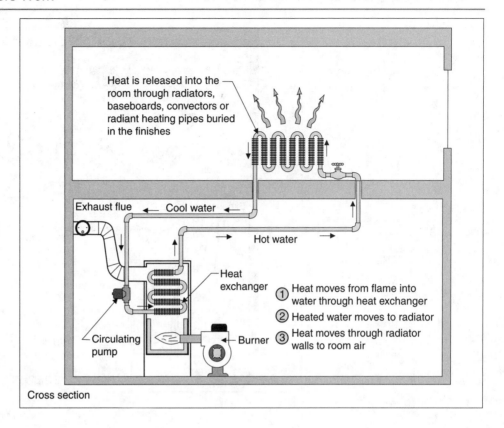

Cross section

Water Circulates

Just as the air in a forced-air system is recirculated, so is the water in a boiler system. Cool water is brought to the boiler, heated, and sent to the radiators. The cool water is returned from the radiators through the piping system, to be warmed again by the heat exchanger.

1.1.3   Heat Transfer Methods

Both furnaces and boilers use conduction to transfer heat from the fire side to the air or water side of the heat exchanger. Furnaces use primarily convection from that point on. Boilers use convection, conduction, and radiation in the distribution system.

Convection

Boilers use convection in two different ways to get heat into a room. Convection helps to move the water through the piping system. Warm water tends to rise and cool water tends to fall, since it's heavier. Gravity water heating systems rely exclusively on convection to move water through the piping system.

Convective Loops

Boilers also use convection to transfer heat from the radiators into the rooms. Radiators are designed to heat the air in the room. They do this by drawing cool air in at the bottom, warming the air as it passes over the radiator, and discharging the heated air at the top (Figure 1.2). This sets up convective loops of air movement within a room.

Conduction

Boiler systems use conduction to transfer heat from the water into the metal radiators or convectors. This is an extra step in heat transfer we don't find with warm-air furnaces.

FIGURE 1.2   How Radiators Heat the Air Through Convection

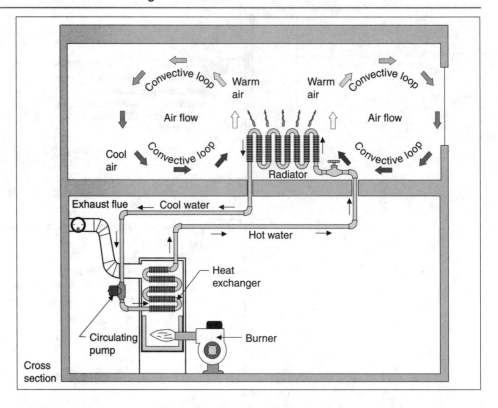

Radiation

Less Important than Convection

Radiators radiate heat in all directions into the room, and, unfortunately, into the exterior wall that they are close to. Any warm body radiates heat in all directions to its cooler surroundings. You might think that radiation is the main method of heat transfer for radiators, because of their name. In fact, radiation is less important than convection. This isn't important from a theoretical standpoint but does have a practical impact. Radiators enclosed in covers that restrict the airflow across the radiators don't work as well as radiators that have unobstructed air movement (Figure 1.3).

Although we've been talking about radiators, this applies to convectors and baseboards as well.

1.1.4   Similarities Between Furnaces and Boilers

Furnaces and boilers both have—

1. Burners, fuel supplies, and combustion controls
2. Combustion air requirements.
3. Venting systems
4. Heat exchangers
5. Cabinets
6. High-temperature limit switches
7. Thermostats

F I G U R E 1.3   Radiator Covers

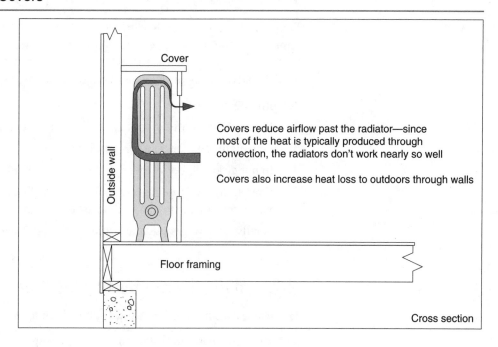

1.1.5   **Differences Between Boilers and Furnaces**

The differences between boilers and furnaces that are important to home inspectors are:

1. Boilers have pipes. Furnaces have ducts.

2. Boilers have radiators, convectors, or radiant pipes. Furnaces have registers and grills.

3. Boilers have pumps instead of fans, with pump controls instead of fan controls.

4. Boilers do not have air filters or electronic air cleaners.

5. Boilers cannot have central air conditioning or humidification systems added.

6. Boilers are connected to the house plumbing system (to provide water to the boiler system).

7. There is a control to maintain the boiler water pressure at a desired level.

8. There is often a device to keep the boiler water from getting back into our drinking water.

9. Boilers have a safety device (pressure-relief valve) to prevent water pressure building up in the boiler system.

10. Boilers have an expansion tank to allow the water to expand without creating high pressures when the water heats up.

11. Some boilers have a safety device designed to turn the boiler off if the water level is too low.

Throughout this section, we will look at the components that are different from furnaces.

We will talk about these components in three groups:

1. The heat exchanger

2. The controls

3. The distribution system

1.1.6   Advantages of Hot Water Heating Systems

People argue about whether furnaces or boilers are better. We think that both systems have their advantages, and you will never tell a client to replace one heating system for another, unless there are special circumstances.

The advantages of hot water heating systems are that they—

1. provide even heat
2. do not create drafts in rooms, so the rooms tend to be more comfortable
3. are usually quieter than forced-air systems
4. do not circulate odors through the home like a forced-air system
5. have piping that requires less room in walls, floors, and ceilings than ducts—this means fewer and smaller bulkheads built into rooms
6. usually have boilers that are smaller than furnaces of equivalent capacity

1.1.7   Disadvantages of Hot Water Heat

Hot water heating has the following disadvantages:

1. It's more costly to install and service compared with forced-air furnaces.
2. It's more difficult to add central air conditioning, humidifying, and filtering equipment to a home.
3. There is a greater selection of furnaces on the market than boilers. This is especially true at the high-efficiency end of the spectrum.
4. Radiators take up more space in rooms than heating registers.
5. A leak in a hot water system usually means water damage. A leak in a supply or return duct system does no damage.

The bottom line is that hot water heating is a good system. Conversion of any heating system is expensive and disruptive.

One Special Disadvantage

Common Safety Issues

Safety is always a consideration on heating systems. Boilers and furnaces both have safety issues regarding the handling, burning, and exhausting of fuels. In this sense, they are similar.

Explosion Hazard

Boilers have an additional safety concern. If pressurized water is overheated, it can result in a steam explosion. Let's look at how that works.

Water normally boils at 212°F. However, if we pressurize the water in a closed system, it won't boil at 212°F. We can heat the water well past 212° in this closed system, increasing its pressure as the temperature rises. Water at 50 psi boils at 300°F.

Superheated Water

We can get the temperature to 300°F and still the water won't boil. This is **superheated water.** This is important because of what happens when the piping or the boiler fails and the water is released. Let's back up for a second.

High-Pressure Cold Water—No Problem

If you were to take a tank of room temperature water and pressurize it to 200 psi, there would be a tremendous amount of force in that tank. However, if you ruptured the tank with an ice pick, the tank wouldn't blow up. The pressure would release almost immediately, and water would squirt out for a second and then simply leak out through the hole.

High-Pressure Hot Water—Big Problem

If you took a similar tank and built the pressure up, but also heated the water up to 300°F, for example, the results would be very different. The water wouldn't boil, because it is squeezed into the tank under such high pressure.

FIGURE 1.4 Superheated Water

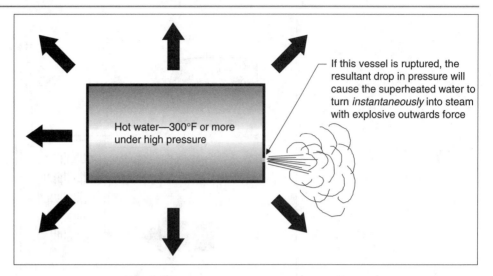

Hot water—300°F or more under high pressure

If this vessel is ruptured, the resultant drop in pressure will cause the superheated water to turn *instantaneously* into steam with explosive outwards force

Since water would like to boil at 212°F at atmospheric pressure, as soon as we release the pressure in that tank, we're going to create steam. When you stick the ice pick into the tank, you relieve the pressure in the same way that we did with the cold water in the tank. The difference is that the superheated water instantaneously boils off into steam as it escapes into the atmosphere (Figure 1.4). It does this so fast that it creates a **steam explosion.**

Steam Explosions

A water heater can easily be shot 300 or 400 feet as the pressure is released. The tank and/or piping forms a deadly projectile. A boiler or tank in the basement of the house, for example, can easily go straight up through a three-story house and have energy left over after it goes through the roof. Obviously, this has the potential to kill someone.

As we talk about hot water heating systems, we'll discuss some safety controls that prevent a superheated water situation and a steam explosion.

1.2   HEAT EXCHANGERS

Just as the heat exchanger is the heart of the furnace, it's also the heart of the boiler.

1.2.1   Function, Materials, and Location

Transfer Heat

Heat exchangers in boilers have the same function as heat exchangers in furnaces: they transfer the heat from the fire into the heat transfer medium. With furnaces, the heat transfer medium is air. With boilers, the heat transfer medium is water.

Common materials include cast iron, steel, alloys, and copper.

Above Burner

The heat exchanger is usually located above the burner and sees the products of combustion coming off the burner. At the top of the heat exchanger, the products of combustion are typically directed into the venting system (Figure 1.5).

The cool water typically enters the bottom of the heat exchanger and the heated water leaves from the top.

F I G U R E 1.5   Heat Exchangers

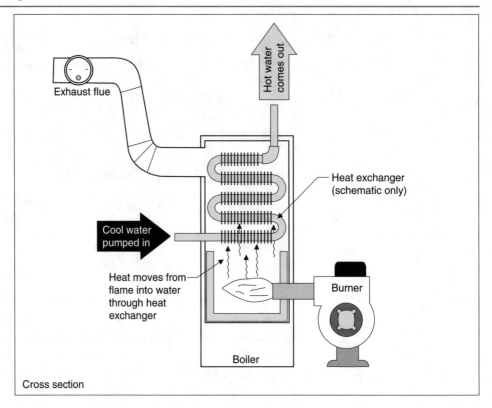

Cross section

1.2.4   Conditions

Failures Are Wet

Heat exchangers on boilers are easier on home inspectors than furnace heat exchangers. When a furnace heat exchanger is cracked or has a hole, it's often difficult to tell. When a boiler heat exchanger has a crack or a hole, it's easy to tell. The water leaks out! It may extinguish the burner or result in water spilling onto the floor around the boiler.

Let's look at the specific problems.

1. Leaks
2. Rust
3. Clogged

Leaks

CAUSES

Heat exchangers on boilers leak because the heat exchanger—

■ is rusted

■ is cracked

■ has poor connections

Rust

Rust is a result of oxygen and water attacking the metal. Rust acts more quickly at higher temperatures, so the environment in a heat exchanger is hostile.

Cracks

Cracks result from the thermal stresses on the heat exchanger over a number of years. Cracks may also be caused by a manufacturing defect.

More Cracks

Cracks may also develop from metal fatigue (perhaps because of overheating, sometimes resulting from not enough water in the boiler, or failure to pump the water through the boiler). A boiler that freezes is also likely to have a cracked heat exchanger.

IMPLICATIONS

Poor Connections

STRATEGY

Dripping and Hissing

Listen as Burner Is Shut Off

Check Outer Jacket

CAUSES

Damp Environment

Chemicals

Don't Drain the Boiler Water in the Summer

Oxygen Causes Rust

A leaking heat exchanger typically has to be replaced. Usually you replace the whole boiler when you have to replace the heat exchanger. There are some exceptions, but for the most part, it's safe to say a new boiler is needed when a heat exchanger leaks.

One exception might be if it is a connection problem. Sometimes sections of heat exchangers are not tightened up securely. Sometimes gaskets fail. In most cases, you won't know and should describe the leaking as a potentially serious problem.

Look for water. Sometimes it's obvious, but sometimes the leak is quite small and only opens when the heating system is firing.

One trick is to look inside the burner compartment at as much of the heat exchanger as you can see just after the burner shuts off. Look for dripping water and listen for the hissing sound of water hitting the hot combustion chamber components (refractory, for example) and boiling off into steam.

Sometimes when you open the burner compartment just after the burner shuts off, you'll see a little puff of steam coming out. This generally means that the heat exchanger has one or more small leaks, allowing water to get through the heat exchanger and into the combustion chamber.

Don't forget to look at the outside jacket of the boiler. Especially on older cast iron and steam boilers, the jacket is part of the heat exchanger. Look for leaks here too. If it is at a seam, it may only be a gasket problem.

Rust

Rust is often caused by condensation from the exhaust products. It's a common cause of corrosion and early failure of heat exchangers, particularly on modern boilers that are substantially oversized.

Rust may also result from a damp environment that a boiler may find itself in such as a chronically wet basement or crawl space.

Common household chemicals can rust furnace or boiler heat exchangers quickly. These include—

- bleaches
- swimming pool chemicals
- muriatic and hydrochloric acid
- aerosol sprays (eg, hair spray)
- deicing salts
- water softener salts
- paint strippers
- glues, cements, and other adhesives

One side of the boiler is always exposed to water and consequently may rust over time.

One cause of rusting heat exchangers is the poor practice of draining the water out of the heating system every summer. Some people think this is good for the heating system because the heat exchanger and pipes won't be attacked by the corrosive water all summer long. They also suggest that flushing the water is a good thing.

The reality is that the same water should remain in the boiler year after year. The amount of oxygen available to corrode the cast iron or steel diminishes in a closed system and the water becomes chemically inert over time. Exposing the metal to oxygen in the air is a bad thing. That's exactly what you do if you drain the water out of the system.

Oxygen in Water

Adding new oxygen in fresh water is also a bad thing. That's what you do if you flush the system. Therefore, a better practice is to keep the same water in the system year after year to minimize rust on the heat exchanger, the pipes, and the radiators.

IMPLICATIONS

Rust on a heat exchanger leads to leaks.

Rust on the fire side of the heat exchanger reduces the boiler's efficiency, increases the heating costs, and may clog the exhaust gas passages, leading to life-threatening spillage of exhaust gases into the home.

STRATEGY

Rust is the enemy of boilers. Look for rust on the external parts of the boiler, at the combustion chamber, and, using a flashlight and mirror, at whatever parts of the heat exchanger are visible. Look for flaking, scaling rust. Look also for pinhole rusting. Pinholes may be small leaks that scab over with rust scale intermittently; however, they usually mean the heat exchanger is near the end of its life.

Watch for corrosive household chemicals stored near the boiler. These can rust the heat exchanger.

Be Gentle

We don't recommend that you poke aggressively at rust on a heat exchanger with a screwdriver, for example. You may end up with an embarrassing amount of water where it doesn't belong.

Turn Boiler off

If you're going to poke around inside combustion chambers and heat exchangers, you don't want the boiler to come on. Many home inspectors shut the power off before venturing into a boiler. We think that's a good idea. An equally good idea is to turn it back on when you're done!

Careful with Copper Tube Boilers

Typically, you can't get a good look at a boiler heat exchanger without dimantling the system, going well beyond our standards. However, one look at a copper-tube heat exchanger can tell you a great deal. These systems are susceptible to corrosion on the fire side of the heat exchanger, typically because of condensation in the exhaust products (Figure 1.6).

Overheated Heat Exchanger

There is also a potential problem with copper-tube boilers overheating. The copper tubing is relatively thin. It's good at transferring heat from the side to the water. However, if the water inside the tubes gets too hot, the copper will overheat and fail prematurely.

Pump Provides Cooling Water

Copper-tube boilers have a pump that pushes water past the heat exchanger quickly. The total water capacity of a copper-tube heat exchanger is only a few gallons. Many of the old, larger, cast-iron heat exchangers have water capacities in the tens of gallons.

Pump Must Be on When Boiler on

The pump must keep introducing cool water to the heat exchanger to avoid overheating the copper tubing. These systems often have a control that won't allow the burner to come on unless the pump is working.

When you are looking at a copper-tube boiler, make sure the pump is working when the burner is on.

Clogged

CAUSES

The water side of the heat exchanger can become clogged by debris in the water, corrosion of the heat exchanger walls, or both. You won't get to see this kind of clogging, so we won't talk about it much.

Water-Side Rust or Debris

Fire-Side Soot

Soot may also clog the fire side of the heat exchanger in the exhaust flue passages. This is usually because of poor burner adjustment, a defective burner, or a lack of maintenance.

Fire-Side Rust

Rust can clog the fire side of the heat exchanger too, usually from condensation.

F I G U R E 1.6   Copper-Tube Heat Exchanger

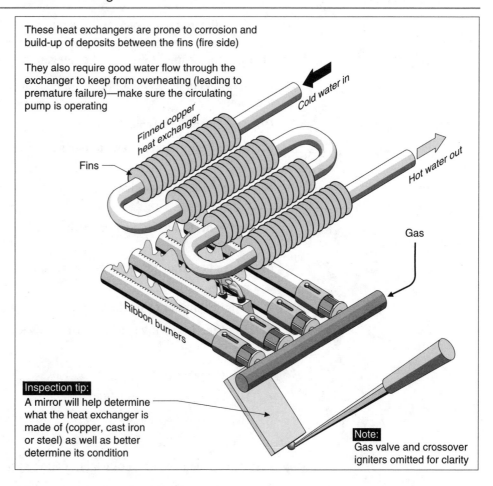

> These heat exchangers are prone to corrosion and build-up of deposits between the fins (fire side)
>
> They also require good water flow through the exchanger to keep from overheating (leading to premature failure)—make sure the circulating pump is operating
>
> *Cold water in*
>
> *Finned copper heat exchanger*
>
> Fins
>
> *Hot water out*
>
> Gas
>
> *Ribbon burners*
>
> Inspection tip:
> A mirror will help determine what the heat exchanger is made of (copper, cast iron or steel) as well as better determine its condition
>
> Note:
> Gas valve and crossover igniters omitted for clarity

IMPLICATIONS

This can result in reduced efficiency of the heating system. A soot buildup on the heat exchanger, for example, restricts the heat transfer, resulting in more heat going straight up the chimney.

It can overheat the heat exchanger if the exhaust flow across the heat exchanger is restricted.

In severe cases, it can lead to spillage of exhaust products back into the house through the burner.

STRATEGY

With a mirror and flashlight, look for black, sooty deposits on the heat exchanger. These should not be seen at all on gas burners, and, although some soot can be expected on an oil burner, watch for measurably thick buildups.

Look for rust on the heat exchanger that can completely obstruct the fins on a copper-tube boiler.

Spillage

Check for spillage of combustion gases as you would on any burner. One cause may be a restricted heat exchanger passage.

Cleaning

Where you have identified a partially clogged or heavily sooted heat exchanger, you're probably looking at a maintenance item rather than a replacement item. This is a far less serious condition in most cases than a leak or severe rusting of a heat exchanger.

CHAPTER REVIEW QUESTIONS

Answer the following questions on a separate sheet of paper, then check your results against the answers provided in Appendix E. If you have trouble with a question, refer back to the chapter to review the relevant material.

1. How do boilers use conduction to transfer heat from the flame to the air in the room?

2. Copper-tube boilers typically have

    a. better heat transfer characteristics and longer lifespans than cast-iron boilers.

    b. better heat transfer characteristics but shorter lifespans than cast-iron boilers.

    c. worse heat transfer characteristics but longer lifespans than cast-iron boilers.

    d. worse heat transfer characteristics and shorter lifespans than cast-iron boilers.

    e. roughly similar characteristics to cast-iron boilers.

3. Which of the following is a similarity between furnaces and boilers?

    a. Piping

    b. A low-level safety device

    c. High-temperature limit switches

    d. Backflow preventers

    e. A pressure-relief valve

4. List five advantages of a hot water heating system.

5. List five disadvantages of a hot water heating system.

6. Explain briefly how we can get superheated water in a hydronic heating system.

7. Heat exchanger diagnosis on boilers is easier than on furnaces because the heat exchanger will leak when it has failed.

    True   False

8. Explain briefly why you don't want to drain the zboiler water in the summer.

KEY TERMS

superheated water   steam explosion

CHAPTER

CONTROLS

LEARNING OBJECTIVES

At the end of this chapter you should be able to:

■ list and describe in one sentence the function of the four types of automatic safety controls

■ list 15 problems found with automatic safety controls

■ describe eight normal operating controls

■ list the common problems found with these operating controls

2.1 OVERVIEW

As we discuss boiler controls, we will assume we have a closed, forced-water system with a pump. This is the most common system and also has the most complex controls. We won't discuss thermostats, since we assume you are familiar with them from your study of gas and/or oil furnaces.

Safety Controls and Operating Controls

There are two very different types of controls on a boiler. Safety controls do what their name suggests: they help make the system safe. Operating controls help the system function efficiently to provide comfortable heat.

Many Variations

There are many ways boilers can be controlled, and we won't include all of them here. We will talk about the most common.

In this section we'll look at four safety controls:

1. Pressure-relief valve

2. High-temperature limit (aquastat)

3. Low-water cutout

4. Backflow preventer

We will also look at eight operating controls:

1. Pressure-reducing valve

2. Automatic air vent

3. Primary control

4. Pump control

5. Zone controls

6. Outdoor air thermostat

7. Flow control valve

8. Isolating valve

For each control, we'll talk about what it does and where it's located. We'll look at what can go wrong with each.

2.2 PRESSURE-RELIEF VALVE

Function

This is the most important safety device on a boiler. This valve prevents the pressure in a boiler system from building beyond 30 psi. We talked about superheated water and steam explosions. The **pressure-relief valve** prevents high pressures, with or without high temperatures (Figure 2.1).

Normal Operating Pressures

The normal operating pressure in a boiler is 12 to 15 psi. The pressure-relief valve, set to relieve at 30 psi, allows pressure to build up with normal heating of the boiler. However, it does not allow the system pressure to get over 30 psi.

Location

The pressure-relief valve is usually located at or near the top of the boiler and is piped down to a discharge point, typically 6 to 12 inches above the floor level.

Don't Test

The Standards do not require us to test safety controls. We do not recommend that you test the pressure-relief valve, although there is a test lever that can be raised. When you raise the lever to test the valve, you actually open the valve and allow water to flow past. The valve often will not reset properly because of some dirt or an internal problem with the valve. Water spilling out onto the floor of the boiler room means an emergency service call, very likely at your expense.

F I G U R E 2.1   Pressure-Relief Valve

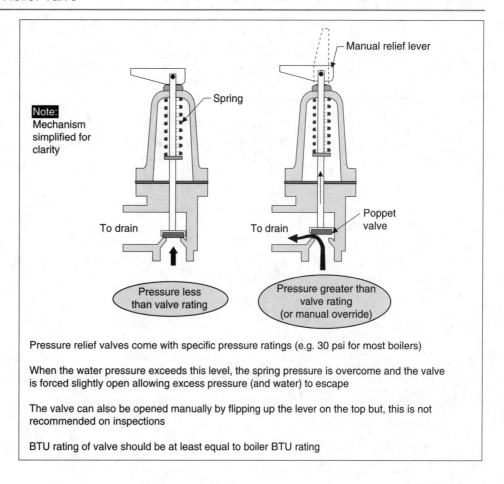

Pressure relief valves come with specific pressure ratings (e.g. 30 psi for most boilers)

When the water pressure exceeds this level, the spring pressure is overcome and the valve is forced slightly open allowing excess pressure (and water) to escape

The valve can also be opened manually by flipping up the lever on the top but, this is not recommended on inspections

BTU rating of valve should be at least equal to boiler BTU rating

Be Consistent

Those of you with special training as heating service people may wish to consider testing safety devices such as pressure-relief valves, but if you are going to do this, you should consider the consistency of your inspection. Are you going into more depth in the heating system because of special expertise you have? If so, are you making it clear to your client that you are doing a more in-depth inspection on the heating system than on other systems? Will your client be misled by your depth of inspection on the heating system and assume it extends to all systems? You can see your liability here.

2.2.1 Conditions

Let's assume we won't be testing safety controls, and look at some of the problems you can identify (Figure 2.2).

1. Missing
2. Wrong size
3. Wrong pressure setting
4. Poor location
5. No piped extension
6. Pipe too small
7. Pipe threaded, capped, or corroded at the bottom
8. Pipe dripping or leaking

F I G U R E 2.2   Inspecting Pressure-Relief Valves

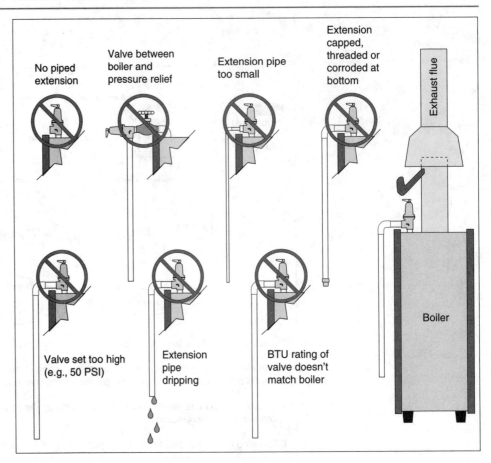

No piped extension	Valve between boiler and pressure relief	Extension pipe too small	Extension capped, threaded or corroded at bottom

Exhaust flue

Boiler

Valve set too high (e.g., 50 PSI)

Extension pipe dripping

BTU rating of valve doesn't match boiler

IMPLICATION

The implication of all of these issues is life safety, unless otherwise stated.

Missing

All closed hot water systems should have a pressure-relief valve. We will talk about open systems later, but they are not common. Recommend further investigation wherever you don't see a pressure-relief valve, unless you are sure it is not needed.

CAUSE

This is an installation issue.

STRATEGY

Look for a valve at or near the top of the boiler (Figure 2.3). It can be attached to the boiler or to the piping. The valve itself can be brass or steel. It usually has a lever on it to allow for testing. It always has a threaded discharge port at the bottom that should be connected to a discharge pipe extending down to near the floor level.

Wrong Size

The pressure-relief valve should be sized properly for the burner. The valve usually has a tag that indicates its BTU/hr capacity. For example, a burner with 100,000 BTU/hr input should not have a 50,000 BTU/hr-rated relief valve.

CAUSE

This is an installation issue.

STRATEGY

Check the rating on the relief valve against the burner input capacity. The relief valve rating should always be equal to or greater than the burner rating.

F I G U R E 2.3   Pressure-Relief Valve Location

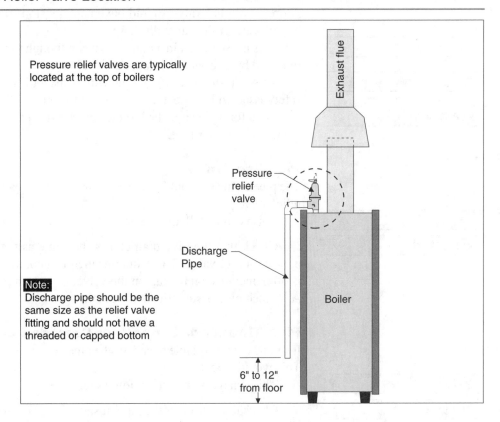

Pressure relief valves are typically located at the top of boilers

Exhaust flue

Pressure relief valve

Discharge Pipe

Note:
Discharge pipe should be the same size as the relief valve fitting and should not have a threaded or capped bottom

Boiler

6" to 12" from floor

Set Wrong

The pressure-relief valve is normally set at 30 psi. Most of these are preset and cannot be adjusted. Some can be adjusted.

This is a service problem.

CAUSE

STRATEGY

Very often, you won't be able to tell what the setting is. However, if you can identify the valve as an adjustable type, or if the valve is rated for more than 30 psi and is not adjustable, you should call for further investigation. The tag on the valve usually indicates its setting.

If the tag says 30 psi, you should be fine. If the tag says 20 to 60 psi, it is adjustable. You won't be able to tell what it is set at. You should call for a specialist to check and either replace the valve or ensure that it is set properly. If the tag on the valve says 60 psi, for example, you should recommend replacement of the valve.

Poor Location

The valve should be located on the top of the boiler or on the piping very close to it (Figure 2.3). The further away from the boiler the valve is placed, the less likely it is to operate quickly and safely.

This is an installation issue.

CAUSE

STRATEGY

Locate the pressure-relief valve. If it's not on or near the top of the boiler, recommend that it be checked during regular servicing. Watch for an isolating valve between the boiler and the relief valve. There should not be one. We don't want to be able to cut off the relief valve from the boiler water pressure.

No Piped Extension

A pressure-relief valve should have an extension so that people won't be scalded by hot water if the valve discharges.

CAUSES

This is usually an installation issue, although the pipe could be inappropriately removed by a service person or even a homeowner.

IMPLICATION

This is a personal safety issue with respect to being scalded rather than a boiler safety issue with respect to a steam explosion.

STRATEGY

Look for a pipe attached to the pressure-relief valve extending down to 6 to 12 inches above floor level.

Pipe Too Small

The pipe diameter should be the same size as the threaded connection on the pressure-relief valve.

CAUSE

This is an installation issue.

STRATEGY

Check that the pipe diameter is the same as the threaded connection on the pressure-relief valve. Three-quarter inch is a common diameter. This information is often included on the tag on the valve. A $1/4$-inch pipe, for example, is too small. A $1/2$-inch pipe is sometimes too small.

Pipe Threaded, Capped, or Corroded at the Bottom

It should not be possible to cap off the piped extension from the pressure-relief valve. This would defeat the valve.

CAUSE

This, again, is an installation issue.

STRATEGY

Check the bottom of the pipe. It should not be threaded. It should not be capped off. Watch for corrosion that may obstruct the pipe at the bottom.

Rust at Bottom

It's common for the pressure-relief valve to operate from time to time over the life of the boiler. In many cases, the operation is intermittent and corrosion may develop at the bottom of the discharge pipe, which is often galvanized steel. This corrosion can reduce the pipe diameter and effectively cap it off. Where you see corrosion, recommend investigation and correction.

Pipe Dripping or Leaking

The pipe from the pressure-relief valve should not be dripping. Dripping may mean the valve is defective or set incorrectly or the system has been operating at pressures in excess of 30 psi. The valve seat may also be obstructed so it won't seal. The valve rating may also be too small for the boiler.

CAUSES

Defective Pressure-Reducing Valve

The valve may be operating properly and the system pressure may be too high. There are a number of reasons for this. If the pressure-reducing valve doesn't do its job, it may allow the house plumbing pressure to enter the boiler. House plumbing systems are usually at 40 to 80 psi.

Waterlogged Expansion Tank

In a closed system, the water pressure builds as the water heats. An expansion tank is designed to minimize the pressure rise. If the expansion tank is too small or waterlogged, it can't prevent the pressure rise, and the pressure-relief valve may operate as a result.

Tankless Coil

A dripping pipe from a pressure-relief valve may also indicate a leak in a tankless coil or indirect water heater. These are systems where the plumbing water goes through the boiler to be heated for domestic use. Instead of having a conventional water heater and storage tank, the boiler water heats the water in the plumbing system. If a leak develops in this system, the 50 or 60 psi water from the plumbing system can enter the boiler water. Since the pressure-relief valve is set to discharge at 30 psi, the valve will open.

F I G U R E 2.4   High-Temperature Limit Switch

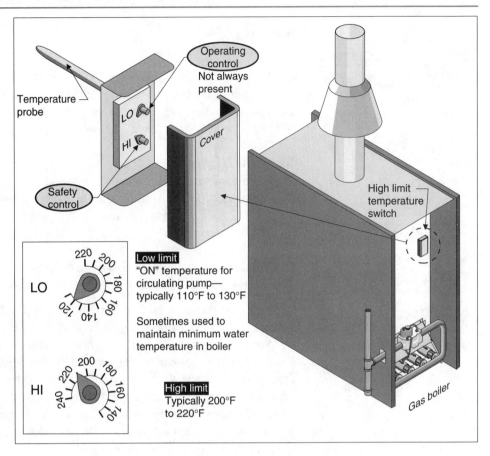

IMPLICATIONS

The implications may be simply replacing the valve or draining a waterlogged expansion tank. However, it is a red flag. Recommend that a service technician investigate and correct the cause of the dripping or leaking.

2.3   HIGH-TEMPERATURE LIMIT SWITCH

This switch performs the same function as the high-temperature limit on a furnace: it shuts off the boiler if the temperature gets too high. This switch is located either in the boiler or in the supply piping just above the boiler (Figure 2.4). It is typically set at 200°F to 220°F. A common setting is 210°F.

On most systems you can look at the **high-temperature limit switch** and see its setting.

2.3.1   Conditions

Common problems include—

1. Missing
2. Set too high
3. Defective or not wired correctly

IMPLICATION

As with pressure-relief valves, the implication for all of these problems is safety.

Missing

CAUSE

This is an installation issue.

STRATEGY

Look for a high-temperature limit switch. You may have to remove the front cover panel of the boiler to locate the limit switch. It may be inside the cabinet on the front of the boiler, or it may be on the hot distribution piping just above the boiler, where the heated water leaves the boiler itself.

Set Too High

Set at 210°F

The high-temperature limit switch is usually set around 210°F. If it is set above this, you should recommend that a service person check the setting. If it is set above 250°F, this is a definite safety problem and you should recommend priority correction.

Defective or not Wired Correctly

CAUSES

This is either a manufacturing or an installation issue.

STRATEGY

Testing Beyond Standards

Home inspectors will not normally know whether the unit operates properly. Testing safety devices goes beyond our Standards.

Some inspectors check the high-temperature limit this way: With the boiler operating, the inspector notes the setting of the high-temperature limit and slowly turns the setting down until the limit switch turns the boiler off. The point at which the limit switch turns the boiler off should be very close to the boiler water temperature, which can be read on the boiler water gauge. If these are roughly the same temperature, the inspector considers the limit switch to be working properly and returns the limit setting to its original position.

Again, we emphasize that this goes beyond a basic home inspection and we are not recommending this test be done.

2.4 LOW-WATER CUTOUT

A **low-water cutout** is a device that shuts off the boiler if the water level is too low. This may happen if the boiler leaks or is drained and then fired. This will overheat and usually crack the heat exchanger, ruining the boiler. Worse, it can generate steam in the piping system if the boiler is partly filled with water. This can be very dangerous.

A low-water cutout is not used on all residential boilers. In our area, it's typically found on boilers with an input capacity of 400,000 BTUs or more. You should determine when, if ever, a low-water cutout is required on residential boilers in your area.

Identifying Them

Low-water cutouts are usually easy to identify. They are usually mounted above the boiler and have a piped connection to the bottom and the top of the boiler or piping (Figure 2.5). The body of the low-water cutout is often fairly large (larger than a grapefruit), and there is electrical wiring running to the unit. If a nametag is visible, it is usually labeled "low-water cutout." Some have isolating valves so they can be serviced without draining the boilers.

FIGURE 2.5 Low-Water Cutout

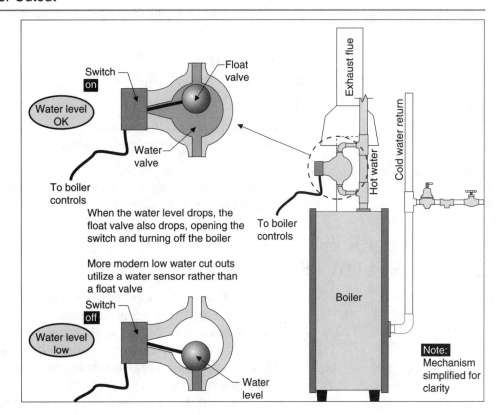

2.4.1 Conditions

Common problems with low-water cutouts include

1. Missing
2. Leaking
3. Inoperative

These conditions all have similar safety implications.

IMPLICATIONS

Missing

As low-water cutouts are not needed on all residential boilers, you should know at what level, if any, they are needed in your area.

CAUSE

If a low-water cutout is missing and should have been provided, this is an installation issue.

STRATEGY

Look for a low-water cutout mounted on the side of the boiler. If it's not there and is needed, point that out.

Leaking

CAUSES

This may be from wear-and-tear, poor maintenance, mechanical damage, or corrosion.

STRATEGY

Look for evidence of leakage around the low-water cutout and its pipe connections. Obviously, any leakage around a boiler should be noted. Repairs should be recommended.

CAUSES

Inoperative

A low-water cutout may be inoperative because it is

- it is defective
- it is clogged
- it is installed incorrectly
- it is wired incorrectly
- an isolating valve below the cutout is closed, preventing it from losing its water, even if the boiler loses its water

STRATEGY

Other than being able to identify closed isolating valves, you normally won't be able to tell whether the low-water cutout is working properly. Again, testing safety controls goes beyond our scope.

2.5 BACKFLOW PREVENTER

The **backflow preventer** stops the boiler water from getting back into the drinking water (Figure 2.6). The boiler is connected to the house plumbing system so that we can add water to the boiler. On old systems, this is done manually by opening a valve to allow more water into the boiler system when it was needed.

Modern systems use a **pressure-reducing valve** to add water automatically into the boiler system to maintain its pressure at 12 to 15 psi. Some have a built-in check valve to prevent backflow. Because this pressure-reducing valve (also known as an

FIGURE 2.6 Backflow Preventer

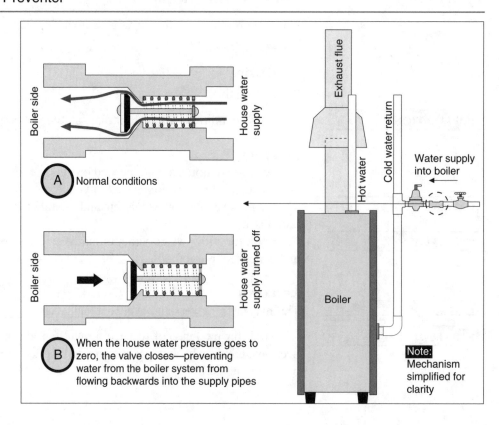

automatic water makeup valve) can fail, like any mechanical device, many jurisdictions require a backflow preventer. This is effectively a double-check valve that prevents water from flowing back out of the boiler system into the house plumbing piping. You don't want to drink water that's been in a boiler system for a number of years.

How Could Backflow Ever Occur?

The house plumbing system is typically at 60 psi and the boiler is typically at 12 to 15 psi. How could water ever flow from the boiler system into the plumbing system? It's fairly common to have the water shut off from time to time to replace a washer, fix a leak, change a water heater or add a dishwasher. Without a backflow preventer, it's possible for the water to flow out of the boiler system into the plumbing system when the pressure in the plumbing system is close to zero.

Not all jurisdictions require backflow preventers. You should check to see whether it's necessary in your area.

2.5.1   Location

The backflow preventer is usually next to the pressure-reducing valve (which we'll look at shortly) on the short run of connecting piping that joins the cold water supply piping from the plumbing to the boiler itself (Figure 2.7).

F I G U R E 2.7   Pressure-Reducing Valve Location

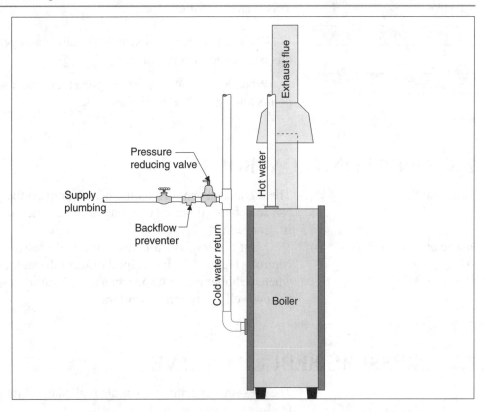

2.5.2   Conditions

1. Missing
2. Leaking
3. Installed backwards

Missing

CAUSE

This is an installation issue. In jurisdictions where backflow preventers are required, you should recognize that they aren't always required on all systems retroactively. Often, they're only required with new installations. While you may want to recommend it as an improvement, its absence is not necessarily a mistake.

IMPLICATION

The implication is a life safety issue. Putting foul water into our drinking water can obviously make people sick, at the very least.

STRATEGY

Know whether backflow preventers are required and under what circumstances. Look for them and make the appropriate recommendations.

Leaking

CAUSE

A leaking backflow preventer may be caused by poor installation, mechanical damage (vibration), etc.

IMPLICATIONS

In most cases, this is a nuisance. In some cases, it can allow backflow.

STRATEGY

Look for leaks and recommend that they be corrected.

Installed Backwards

CAUSE

This is an installation issue.

IMPLICATIONS

The safety benefit is lost and the boiler can't get any makeup water. Therefore, this isn't a common problem.

STRATEGY

When looking at a backflow preventer, make sure that the arrow on the valve points toward the boiler (Figure 2.8).

2.6   OPERATING CONTROLS

Thermostat

The thermostat can turn on the burner, turn on the pump, or open a zone valve. It can sometimes do more than one of these functions, depending on how the boiler is arranged.

Temperature and Pressure Gauge

Most boilers have a temperature and pressure gauge, although these are not controls (Figure 2.9). It is helpful to know the temperature and pressure of the water when the boiler is at rest and when it is operating at steady state. This provides clues to how well the system is working.

2.7   PRESSURE-REDUCING VALVE

The pressure-reducing valve is also called the automatic water makeup valve or the feed-water pressure regulator.

The pressure-reducing valve connects the house plumbing supply system to the boiler water. It is designed to automatically maintain an adequate amount of water in the boiler at the desired pressure (12 to 15 psi).

F I G U R E 2.8   Backflow Preventer Installed Backwards

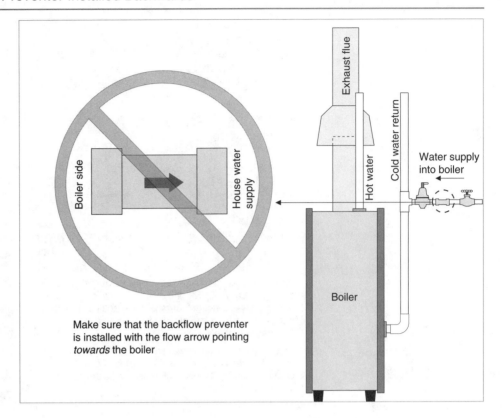

Make sure that the backflow preventer
is installed with the flow arrow pointing
towards the boiler

F I G U R E 2.9   Temperature and Pressure Gauge

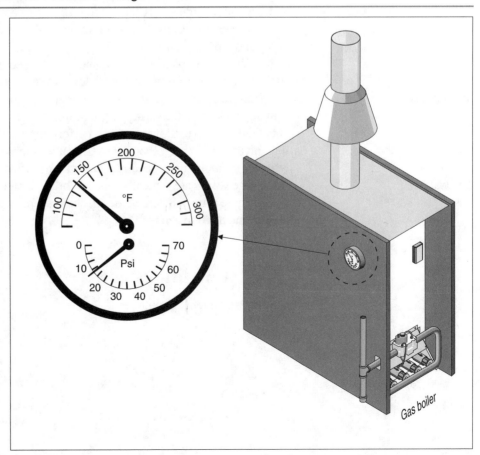

F I G U R E 2.10   Pressure-Reducing Valve

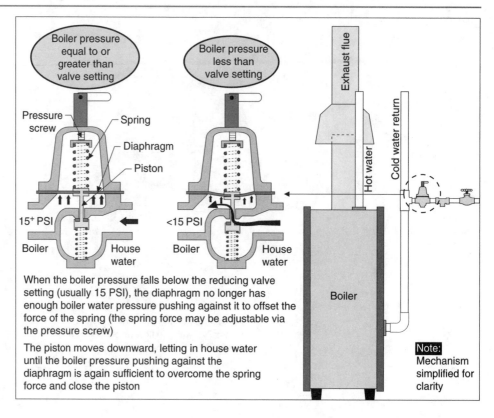

Location

The valve is typically on a short connector pipe between the plumbing system and the boiler (Figure 2.10). It is often close to a backflow preventer. The pressure-reducing valve can also be part of an assembly that includes a pressure-reducing valve and a pressure-relief valve.

When these two units are combined into one component, they should be installed so that the pressure-relief valve is closer to the boiler (Figure 2.11).

Integral Check Valve

Some pressure-reducing valves have an integral check valve that prevents water flowing back from the heating system into the plumbing system. We talked earlier about a distinct backflow preventer performing this function. Some pressure-reducing valves can do it on their own. Check in your area to see what is common and whether municipalities require a separate backflow preventer.

Materials

These valves are typically made of brass or steel and are very often shaped like a bell. There is no discharge pipe attached to a pressure-reducing valve because they are not intended to relieve water.

2.7.1   Conditions

Common problems include—

1. Set too low
2. Missing
3. Inoperative
4. Leaking
5. Installed backwards

F I G U R E 2.11   Combined Pressure-Reducing Valve and Pressure-Relief Valve

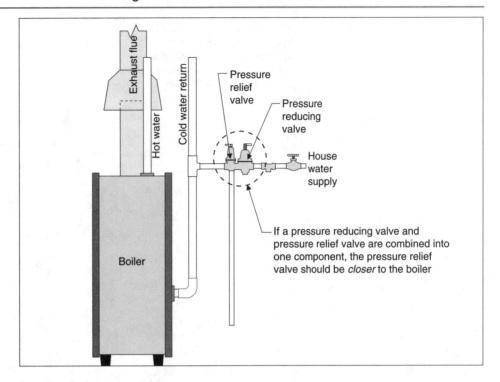

Set Too Low

CAUSE

Tall House Problems

Pressure-reducing valves are usually factory-set at between 12 and 15 psi. Some are adjustable within this range and beyond (10 to 25 psi range is common).

They are rarely faulty but may be set too low because of the house configuration. A tall three-story house with a basement may require a pressure-reducing valve set at more than 12 psi. The pressure at the boiler has to push water up to the top of the heating system. If the radiators on the upper floor are not filled with water, these rooms will be cold.

Pressure Used To Elevate Water

A pressure of 1 psi can push water up roughly 2.31 feet (about 28 inches). A pressure of 10 psi can push a column of water up 23.1 feet; 12 psi (commonly available at pressure-reducing valves) can push water up (12 times 2.31) about 28 feet. A pressure of 15 psi (the maximum for most pressure-reducing valves) can push water up about 34$^1/_2$ feet.

Total Height of System

Let's look at that three-story house. From the pressure-reducing valve to the basement ceiling might be 5 feet. The first floor may be 1 foot above the basement ceiling. If the height of the first floor is 11 feet (typical of Victorian homes), we are now 17 feet above the pressure-reducing valve.

32 Feet above Boiler

Moving up through the 1-foot thick floor system and then through a 10-foot tall second floor, adds another 11 feet. Now we're 28 feet above the pressure-reducing valve. Moving through the 1-foot thick third floor and approximately 3 feet above the floor to the top of the radiator adds another 4 feet. This brings us up to 32 feet.

12 psi Won't Push Water High Enough

As you can see, if the pressure-reducing valve is set at 12 psi (good for 28 feet), there may not be enough water pressure to fill the third-floor radiators (Figure 2.12). Ideally, there should be enough pressure to fill the third-floor radiators and have at least 2 or 3 psi left over. If the valve is set at 15 psi (good for 34$^1/_2$ feet), we should be all right, just barely.

IMPLICATIONS

The top floor of the house will be cold if the radiators will not fill with water.

F I G U R E 2.12 Pressure Set Too Low

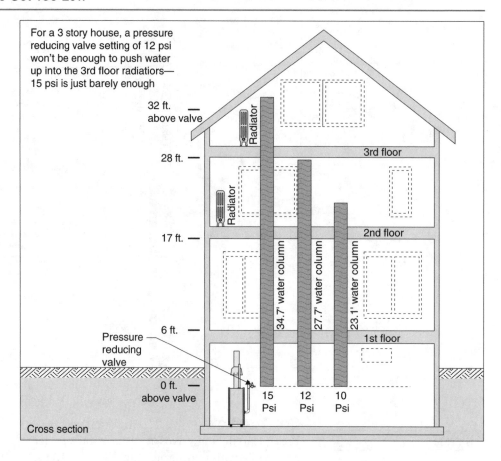

For a 3 story house, a pressure reducing valve setting of 12 psi won't be enough to push water up into the 3rd floor radiatiors— 15 psi is just barely enough

32 ft. above valve
28 ft.
17 ft.
6 ft.
0 ft. above valve

Radiator
Radiator
3rd floor
2nd floor
1st floor

34.7' water column
27.7' water column
23.1' water column

Pressure reducing valve

15 Psi   12 Psi   10 Psi

Cross section

Don't Operate the Bleed Valves

When the system is operating, run your hand along the top floor radiators from bottom to top. If the radiator is not full, you can feel a distinct temperature change on the radiator surface when you get above the water level. The cast iron will feel much cooler.

We'll talk about radiators in a little bit, but you may have already noticed an air bleed valve at one end of the top of the radiator (Figure 2.13). This allows you to get rid of any air that has accumulated in the system. Some home inspectors go beyond the Standards and operate this bleed valve. This is risky because the valve may not close properly and you may cause a leak. The advantage of doing this is that you can find out whether the water does fill the radiator. When you open the valve, you may get water out immediately. This tells you that the radiator is full and everything is fine.

You may get a rush of air, and eventually water, out of the valve. This is also fine. You have bled some air out of the system and actually improved the efficiency somewhat. The radiator is now filled with water.

You may get air coming out of the bleed valve for a while and then nothing. In this case, you have relieved the little bit of air pressure in the radiator, but since you got no water, it's possible the radiator isn't full of water. There is one other possibility. The bleed valve may be obstructed so that neither air nor water can get through the valve itself.

Again, we do not recommend operating radiator bleed valves because of the risk of leakage and the possibility of not getting the valve closed properly.

F I G U R E 2.13   Don't Operate Air Bleed Valve

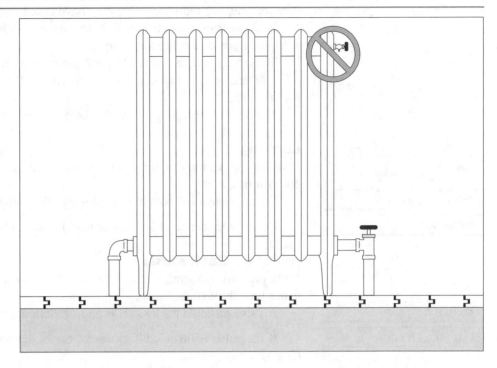

Missing

A missing pressure-reducing valve is an installation issue.

Pressure-reducing valves are not absolutely necessary. They are an operating convenience. You can fill a boiler manually by opening a valve that connects the plumbing system to the heating system.

A pressure-reducing valve is a plus, but not a necessity. If you advise adding one, make it clear that it's an improvement rather than a repair.

Inoperative

The pressure-reducing valve can be inoperative two different ways.

1. The pressure-reducing valve may be obstructed or defective and no water may get through into the boiler.

2. The pressure-reducing valve may have failed and the water pressure in the boiler system may be too high.

There may be a problem with the valve, or dirt may be obstructing the valve. It's also remotely possible that the valve was installed backwards.

If the pressure-reducing valve doesn't allow enough water through, the house won't get warm enough, especially on the upper floors. The boiler will eventually run short of water and probably shut down on high-temperature limit or low-water cutout.

If too much pressure is allowed through, the pressure-relief valve will operate constantly. If the pressure-relief valve isn't working or is missing, there is a risk of a pressure build-up and a steam explosion.

The best way to determine whether the pressure-reducing valve is operating properly is to look at the temperature and pressure gauge on the boiler. When the boiler is cold, the pressure should be 12 to 15 psi. If the pressure is much lower than

CAUSE

IMPLICATION

STRATEGY

CAUSES

IMPLICATIONS

STRATEGY

this, there may not be enough water in the system. If the pressure range is above this, the pressure-reducing valve may have failed.

High pressure may also result in the pressure-relief valve operating. Watch for a dripping pressure-relief valve pipe.

There are other causes for the boiler pressure being too high and the pressure-relief valve dripping, including an expansion tank that is waterlogged or undersized, for example.

The temperature gauge may also be defective.

Leaking

CAUSES

Leaking valves may be the result of poor installation, mechanical damage, or corrosion.

IMPLICATIONS

Water damage and possible shut down of the heating system are the implications.

STRATEGY

Look for evidence of leakage around the pressure-reducing valve.

Installed Backwards

Most pressure-reducing valves have an arrow indicating the proper direction of water flow through the valve.

CAUSE

A valve installed backwards is an installation issue.

IMPLICATIONS

If the valve is installed backwards, the boiler will not get any makeup water (Figure 2.14).

A more serious implication is in the case of the combination pressure-reducing valve and pressure-relief valve. If the assembly is installed backwards, the boiler pressure-relief valve will be upstream of (before) the pressure-reducing valve. This puts it too far away from the boiler, and this important safety device may be compromised.

F I G U R E 2.14 Pressure-Reducing/Relief Valve Installed Backwards

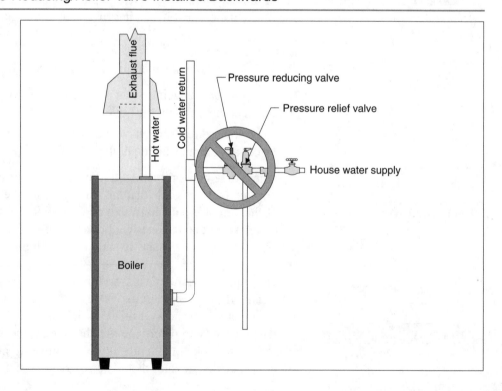

There is an arrow on the body of the valve. The arrow should point to the boiler.

2.8 AIR VENT

Air vents can be manual or automatic. They are sometimes called air eliminators. Their function is to get rid of air in the water. Boiler air vents are typically located at the top of the boiler. Automatic vents are often chromed and bell shaped.

Option

An air vent is not mandatory, although some boilers come with an integral vent. Some boiler designs are more prone to trapping air within the boiler than others. Most boilers with diaphragm-type expansion tanks have vents.

Protect Pumps

Air vents are more important on boilers with pumps. Pumps can be damaged by air pockets. Air vents are sometimes used with air scoops (air separators). These are devices built into the piping system, designed to create an area of low water velocity so air bubbles can rise to the surface (Figure 2.15). They then usually escape through an air vent or into the expansion tank.

Conventional expansion tanks, located above boilers, can collect the air. Tanks with diaphragms (bladders) have no air/water contact, so they need an air vent. We talked briefly about the bleed valves on radiators throughout the system. These are also air vents on the distribution side, although we don't call them vents.

F I G U R E 2.15 Air Separators

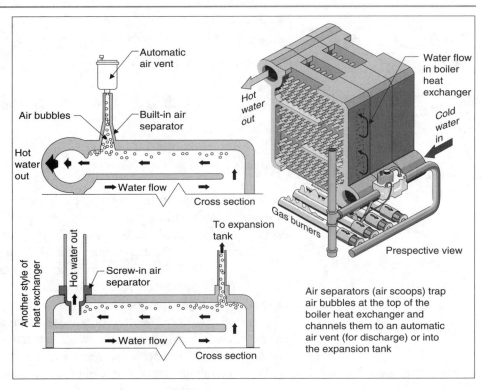

2.8.1 Conditions

Look for the following air vent problems during your inspection:

1. Missing
2. Inoperative
3. Leaking

Missing

CAUSES

A missing air vent is either a design issue on the boiler itself or an installation issue.

IMPLICATIONS

Air trapped in the water will disrupt the efficiency to some extent and may lead to localized overheating of the heat exchanger. However, determining whether this is a problem on any given boiler is beyond the scope of a home inspection.

STRATEGY

Note the presence of an air vent, but do not criticize the absence of one. If a diaphragm-type expansion tank is noted, recommend that a service person evaluate the need for an air vent.

Inoperative

CAUSES

An air vent may be inoperative because of a manufacturing problem, corrosion, poor adjustment, or obstruction of the air passage.

IMPLICATION

Obviously, an inoperative air vent can't do its job.

STRATEGY

Operational testing of an air vent is not part of the home inspection. If the vent is obviously corroded, you may suspect that it is inoperative and recommend servicing. In any case, this is not a serious boiler problem.

Leaking

CAUSES

Leaks may be caused by poor connection, corrosion, or, mechanical damage.

IMPLICATIONS

Water damage and possible loss of adequate water in the boiler are the implications.

STRATEGY

Watch for evidence of water leakage around the air vent.

2.9 PRIMARY CONTROL

The low-temperature limit, operating control aquastat, or **primary control** as it is sometimes called, is designed to keep the water in the boiler hot so that it can respond quickly to a call for heat (Figure 2.16). Large cast-iron boilers, in particular, take some time to heat up if the water is allowed to cool to room temperature. Many systems are designed to keep the water in the boiler at anywhere from 120° to 200°F so that the boiler is ready to respond. A typical setting is 140°F. This minimizes thermal lag in the system.

Primary controls can be strap-on aquastats. This is a brand name that has become generic for control devices that sense water temperature. These can also be immersion-type aquastats with temperature probes in the water itself.

Don't Confuse Terms

We talked about primary controllers or primary controls on oil burners. These are different. The primary control on the burner is an automatic safety device that shuts off the burner if no flame is seen. The boiler primary control just keeps the water warm in standby mode. It's not a safety device.

F I G U R E 2.16 Aquastat—Primary Control

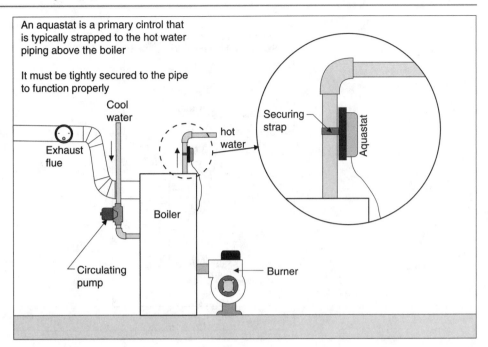

An aquastat is a primary cintrol that is typically strapped to the hot water piping above the boiler

It must be tightly secured to the pipe to function properly

Cool water

Exhaust flue

hot water

Securing strap

Aquastat

Boiler

Circulating pump

Burner

Tankless Water Heaters

Some boilers keep their water hot because domestic hot water is provided by the boiler water as well. Even when the boiler has no demand for heat, the water in the boiler has to be hot so the domestic water can be heated. Some argue against the efficiency of this arrangement, but it is common in some areas.

Not Always Used

Not all systems have a primary control. Many boilers are allowed to cool to room temperature when there is no demand for heat. The smaller steel and copper-tube boilers can heat up more quickly than the old large cast-iron boilers, and so there isn't the same thermal lag built into the system. On these boilers, an operating control is much less important.

Zone Systems

Hot water heating systems with multiple zones often use a primary control to keep the boiler water hot. Various thermostats can activate various zones by turning on a pump or opening a valve. The thermostats on these systems do not activate the burner. The primary control is often the only thing that makes the burner come on and off.

Operating within a Window

The operating control maintains the boiler water temperature within a range of 10°F, for example. The control can be set to have the boiler come on at 180°F and turn off at 190°F, for example.

More than One Approach

We are starting to see that there are different approaches for operating a boiler. The thermostat may turn on the burner to heat the system up. This is the way furnaces work. But now we're talking about a system where the boiler stays hot and the thermostat activates a pump to move the heated water through the house, or opens a zone valve and activates the pump to allow water to move through a part of the house.

If you inspect in an area where hot water heating is common, you will see several control methods. We won't talk about them all, but will include the typical ones. You need to know how systems are normally run in your area.

FIGURE 2.17 Inoperative Aquastat

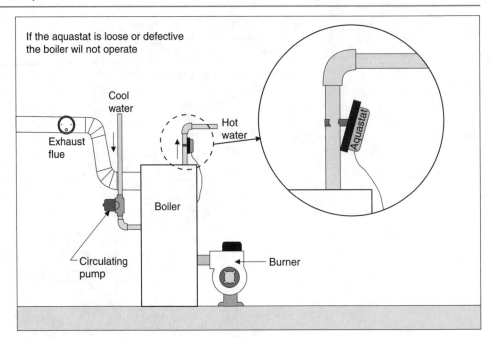

If the aquastat is loose or defective the boiler wil not operate

Cool water

Exhaust flue

Hot water

Aquastat

Boiler

Circulating pump

Burner

2.9.1 Conditions

Primary control problems include the following:

1. Inoperative
2. Set incorrectly

Inoperative

CAUSES

IMPLICATION

STRATEGY

Mechanical or electrical malfunction are common causes of problems. A loose strap-on aquastat is also a cause of inoperative units (Figure 2.17).

If the primary control doesn't work, there will be no heat. This normally results in an emergency service call.

When you are in a house where the boiler is at rest, you will typically turn up the thermostat to test the heating system. If the boiler water is at room temperature and the burner doesn't come on when the thermostat calls for heat, you may suspect a primary control that's malfunctioning. If the pump comes on when the thermostat is turned up but the boiler fails to fire, this reinforces the possibility of a primary control problem.

Don't Troubleshoot

But let's leave it there, before we get too far into troubleshooting. Have a service technician walk you through, if you want to go further.

Set Incorrectly

The set point on most controls can be adjusted easily. The set point can be either too high or too low. Set points are sometimes changed season to season or are tied directly to the outdoor temperature.

This could be a technician adjustment mistake or a homeowner mistake.

CAUSES

IMPLICATIONS

There are different implications to different improper settings. If the primary control is set too high, the boiler water may be near the high-temperature limit.

Keeping water at over 200°F in the boiler is inefficient at best and may overheat the boiler, shortening its life.

Setting the control too low may mean a long wait for heat when the thermostat calls.

Summer Setting

Some primary controls have at their lower end the setting described as *Summer.* Rather than a temperature setting, this setting allows the homeowner or service person to ensure that the boiler won't come on during the warm summer months.

Too High

If the water temperature on the gauge is over 200°F when the boiler is at rest, you may suspect the primary control is set too high. You can usually look at the setting and determine this. In some cases, the setting indicated is not accurate. When the boiler temperature is over 200°F, you should probably recommend servicing, in any case.

Too Low

If the primary control is set too low, the burner may not come on, no matter what you do with the thermostat. If the operating control is set to the Summer position, the burner won't fire because it thinks the water is warm enough.

Beyond the Standards Again

Some inspectors will turn the primary control up to make the burner fire. Again, this is beyond home inspection scope, and for those of you who get into this kind of thing, you should make sure that you reset the control to the point you found it. Again, we recommend not doing this unless you are a qualified service person.

2.10   PUMP CONTROL

Description and Location

The **pump control** is a thermostatic control and can be an aquastat. It looks like the high-temperature limit and the primary control (Figure 2.18). It's mounted in the same location (on the hot distribution piping near the boiler).

Circulator

Incidentally, the pump is often called the circulator. Either term means the same thing. The pump moves the water through the distribution system in a loop, with the water being heated every time it passes the boiler.

Function

The pump control is designed to turn the pump on and off. There are a number of ways that boilers may be set up.

1.   Pump runs continuously

Some pumps run continuously and there is no pump control. The pump is always on. The thermostat turns the burner on when there is a call for heat, and the pump continues to work whether the burner is on or off.

Advantages:
    a. Some people feel that this has the advantage of extending the life of the pump and/or electric motor by eliminating the start-up stresses.
    b. You don't need to buy a control.

Disadvantages:
    a. A disadvantage of this arrangement is that the pump runs throughout the heating season and adds to the electrical costs. Others also feel that the constant operation actually shortens the life of the pump because of bearing wear.
    b. More important, the heat exchanger sees cold water as the burner starts up. This can lead to condensation, which may corrode the heat exchanger.

2.   Pump on when burner is on

The heating system may be designed so that the pump comes on every time the burner comes on. In this case, there will be no pump control either. When the thermostat

F I G U R E 2.18   Pump Control

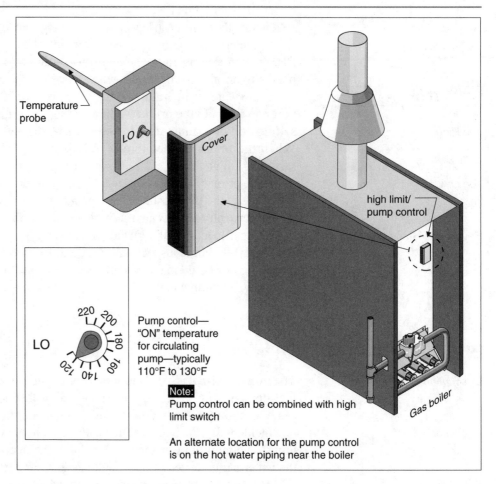

Temperature probe

LO

Cover

high limit/ pump control

220 200 180 160 140 120

LO

Pump control— "ON" temperature for circulating pump—typically 110°F to 130°F

Note:
Pump control can be combined with high limit switch

An alternate location for the pump control is on the hot water piping near the boiler

Gas boiler

calls for heat, the burner is energized and the pump is energized by either the thermostat or burner.

You can see how the advantages and disadvantages will differ from our previous example. The second disadvantage still applies.

3. Pump control turns pump on

On some systems, the pump is designed to come on when the boiler water temperature gets above a set level (eg, 110°F to 140°F). The pump controls tell the pump to come on and off. When the burner shuts off, the pump will continue to run until the boiler water drops below the set point.

In this arrangement, the house thermostat controls the burner. When there is a call for heat, the burner comes on. The thinking here is that there's no point circulating the water through the boiler and distribution system until the water is warm enough to make that worthwhile. This is similar to the furnace fan arrangement. It may help minimize condensation on start-up.

Be Careful!

When you test a hot water heating system, you need to understand all the possible arrangements for the circulator. As you can see, the pump may come on at different times, depending how the system is set up. Don't be too quick to criticize.

2.10.1   Conditions

There are two pump control problems to look for:

1. Inoperative
2. Set incorrectly

Inoperative

If the pump control is inoperative, the pump will never come on or will be on all the time.

This could be a mechanical or an electrical problem.

If the pump does not come on, the heating system will not work comfortably and efficiently.

Some boilers need to have the pump working to supply cool water to the heat exchanger. If the heat exchanger isn't constantly fed with cool water, it can overheat. An inoperative pump can ruin a boiler in this case.

Most boilers that rely on the pump have the burner interlocked so that it can only come on once the pump is on. These systems don't use a pump control, so it shouldn't be an issue.

If the pump runs continuously, the heating system will work, although the electrical consumption will be higher.

The first step is to determine whether there is a pump control. It is usually mounted on the hot supply distribution piping from the boiler, just above the boiler itself. It's often very close to the high-temperature limit switch. Don't confuse the two. The high-temperature limit is normally set at 210°F. The pump control is typically set at 110°F to 140°F.

There may also be a primary control designed to keep the water temperature in the boiler at a set level. This is typically between 160°F and 200°F, although it can be as low as 110°F or 120°F. It's not unusual to see three controls on the piping just above the boiler. The high-temperature limit is the safety control. The pump control and primary control for the burner are normal operating controls.

About the only way to tell whether the pump control is working is to cycle the boiler through and observe whether the pump comes on when the boiler water temperature reaches the set point of the pump control. You should be able to read the setting on the pump control and watch the boiler water temperature rise at the boiler gauge. If the pump does not come on at the set temperature, you may suspect that either the control or the pump is inoperative. Recommend that this be checked by a service person.

If there is a primary control but the pump is always on, the control should be serviced.

Set Incorrectly

The pump control can be set too high or too low.

This may have been done by a technician or by the homeowner.

The implications of setting the pump control too low are simply that the pump will run more often than it otherwise would. Since we've already said that some pumps run continuously through the heating season, this isn't a serious problem. If the setting is too high, the pump won't come on until the boiler water is very hot. It may not come on at all in some cases. This is an efficiency problem and may lead to overheating of the heat exchanger.

CAUSES

IMPLICATIONS

Pump May Have To Run

Burner Interlocked with Pump

STRATEGY

Watch for the Primary Control

Does the Pump Come on?

Is the Pump Always on?

CAUSES

IMPLICATIONS

Too Low, Too High

Again, when you are operating the boiler, watch the pump. Check the setting of the pump control and make sure the pump comes on at an appropriate boiler water temperature. The pump should always be on by the time the boiler water temperature reaches 150°F. It usually comes on around 110°F but can be set as high as 140°F.

2.11 ZONE CONTROL

Large Homes

Large houses with hot water heating often have several zones. Each zone has its own thermostat, which allows the occupants to keep various areas of the house at different temperatures. There are a number of strategies for **zone control.** The zones may be heated by turning pumps on or by activating electric zone control valves. There are advantages to both approaches.

A full discussion of zoned hot water systems is beyond the scope of our program, but we'll discuss the basics here.

Zone Control with Pumps

Pumps can be used to supply heat to various zones. Let's look at a simple two-zone system. There will be a thermostat for each zone. When one thermostat calls for heat, the circulating pump for that zone moves hot water through the distribution piping and radiators for that part of the home (Figure 2.19). The other thermostat is not calling for heat, and its pump will not be moving water.

Thermostat Starts Pump and Maybe Burner

In some cases, when either one of the thermostats calls for heat, the burner also comes on. This means that the thermostat activates the circulator and the burner. In other cases, the boiler water is kept hot by a primary control. In this arrangement, when the thermostat calls for heat, the appropriate pump comes on and moves the hot water through that zone.

F I G U R E 2.19 Zone Control with Pumps

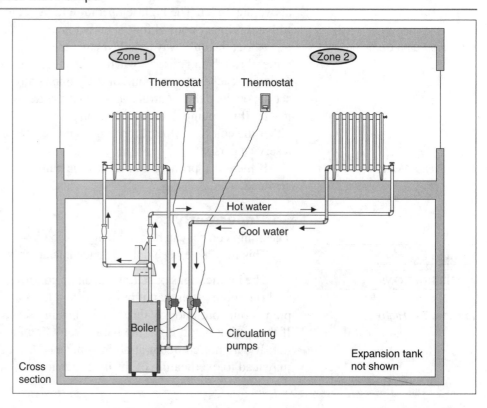

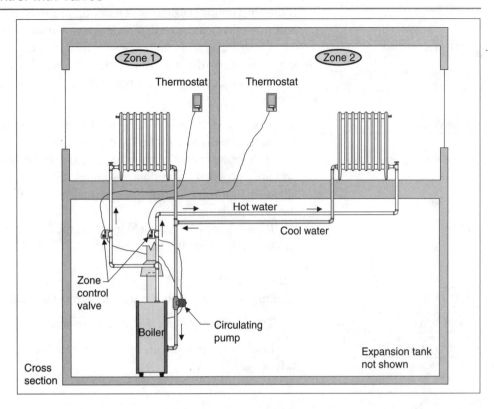

Zone Control with Valves

If both thermostats call for heat, both pumps will work, and hot water will be distributed to all parts of the house.

Let's look at a two-zone system with valves to control the heat. If one thermostat calls for heat, the valve to that zone will be opened and the pump will be activated. The zone valve may turn the pump on after it opens. We don't want the pump working against closed valves since this will damage the pump. Typically, there is just one pump, although there can be two. The thermostat is usually interlocked with both the valve and the pump (Figure 2.20). We don't want the pump running when both zone valves are closed since there is nowhere for the water to go. Bypass loops can be set up, but let's not get too far into this.

When both thermostats call for heat, both zone valves are opened and the circulator delivers hot water to all of the piping and radiators in the home. Again, the boiler may be kept hot with a primary control, or either thermostat could activate the burner.

Multi-zone systems are complex, and it often takes some time to figure out how the system is controlled. In a large home, it can take quite a while just to find all the thermostats.

2.11.1 Conditions

Zone controls may show either of the following problems:

1. Inoperative
2. Leaking

Inoperative

If the zone control system isn't working properly, the pump or valve for that system will not deliver water to that zone, even when the thermostat calls for it.

CAUSES

There are a number of causes for this, including electrical and mechanical problems, and we will not try to troubleshoot this condition.

IMPLICATION

The implication of an inoperative zone control is no heat to that zone of the house.

STRATEGY

Overheat or No Heat

The best strategy is to turn the thermostats up for all the zones and make sure hot water is delivered to the radiators or convectors in the entire house.

If the zone control system has failed and the zone valve is stuck open, there is probably no great harm done, although that part of the house may be too warm. However, if a zone control valve is stuck closed, for example, or cannot be opened, the problem is no heat.

It makes sense to have a helper turn the thermostat up and down. This way, you can see and/or hear the valve operate.

Leaking

Leaking is caused by poor installation, mechanical damage, vibration, or corrosion.

CAUSES

The implications are water damage and, possibly, no heat.

IMPLICATIONS

STRATEGY

Look at all components of the boiler for leakage. This includes pumps and zone valves.

2.12   OUTDOOR-AIR THERMOSTAT

This is an enhancement or alternative to the primary control. Some boilers have a remote sensor that checks the outdoor-air temperature. Again, there are a number of ways that this can be arranged, but some simply have the boiler water kept hot (within a range) when the outdoor temperature drops below a set point (eg, 60°F).

Air Temperature Sensor

The outdoor-air temperature sensor or **outdoor-air thermostat** arrangement recognizes the inefficiency of keeping a large boiler hot when there may not be a call for heat for some time (Figure 2.21). When the outdoor temperatures are high, the boiler is allowed to get cold. As the outdoor temperature drops, the boiler heats up, anticipating a demand for heat from a thermostat.

Commercial and Multi-Family

These systems are used more in commercial than in residential construction, although you may find them in large homes.

More Sophisticated

It's possible to use an outdoor-air temperature sensor to automatically increase the temperature of the boiler water as the outdoor temperature falls. The colder it gets outside, the hotter the water in the boiler is maintained. This ensures that heat will be quickly available when called for by the thermostat.

2.12.1   Condition

The common problem is that the outdoor thermostat is inoperative.

Inoperative

The outdoor-air temperature sensor either turns the burner on to maintain the boiler water temperature within a given range or it doesn't. In many cases, you won't know how the system is arranged. You may not even notice the outdoor-air temperature

FIGURE 2.21   Outdoor-Air Temperature Sensor

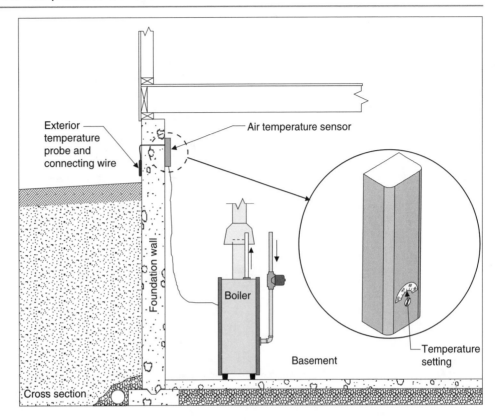

sensor. It's typically a small copper bulb attached to a very small copper line coming into the building and connecting to the boiler controls.

CAUSES

The causes for problems are typically electrical or mechanical.

IMPLICATIONS

Some systems will still work even if the sensor is inoperative. Comfort may be somewhat reduced. Other systems rely entirely on the sensor. If it doesn't work, there will be no heat.

STRATEGY

If you see an outdoor-air temperature sensor, you can explain its function to the client. You should probably recommend that a service person check it during regular servicing.

2.13   FLOW CONTROL VALVE

The **flow control valve** prevents hot water moving through the distribution system when there is no call for heat. It is used on systems where we keep the boiler water hot on standby, and on multi-zone systems.

Water Flows Past Pump Check Valve

With no flow control valve, water will move through the piping by convection. This will overheat the house. The pump (circulator) will not prevent convective flow. The flow control valve can be thought of as a heavy check valve. When the pump comes on, it pushes the valve open so water can move through the system. When the pump stops, the valve closes, and water can't flow through the system. It is typically located on the hot supply distribution piping just past the boiler, although it can be elsewhere (Figure 2.22). There can be more than one. Systems with zone control valves will not use flow control valves, since the zone valves stop the flow when they close.

FIGURE 2.22 Flow Control Valves

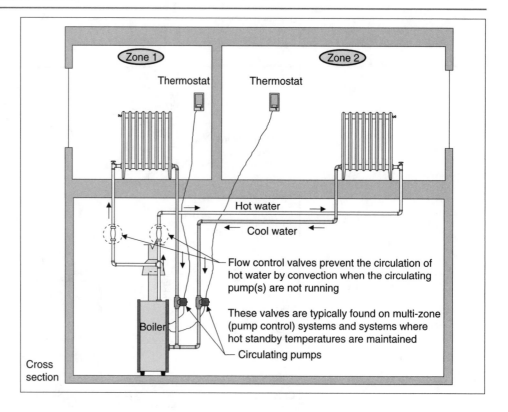

2.13.1   Conditions

Common flow control valve problems include—

1. Leaks
2. Inoperative

Leaks

Like anything connected to a piping system, leaks at connections are possible. We've talked about the causes, implications, and strategies of leaks.

Inoperative

The flow control valve can be stuck open or stuck closed.

This is a mechanical problem.

CAUSE

IMPLICATION

If the valve sticks open (typically because of dirt or corrosion), the house may overheat because water will flow through the system when it's on standby. If the valve sticks closed, there will be no heat for the house or for that zone. The pump and boiler may overheat and shut down on a thermal overload (pump) or high-temperature limit (burner).

2.14   ISOLATING VALVES

Function

Valves are provided on boilers so that various components can be removed for repair or replacement without draining the whole system.

Location

Valves are commonly found—

- on the supply pipe and return pipe near the boiler
- on either side of the pump (circulator)
- on either side of a low-water cutout
- on the pipe connecting the house supplying plumbing to the boiler
- on the supply and return lines of a tankless coil (if used)

More Are Better

Generally speaking, the more valves there are, the better. One valve, strategically placed, can do more than one job. The absence of valves is not a defect, although it is an inconvenience and may result in higher service costs. Don't try to turn any of these valves. Because they aren't used regularly, the packing may be dry and the valve is likely to leak.

2.14.1   Conditions

Isolating valves may exhibit any of these problems:

1. Leak
2. Inoperative
3. Rust or damage

You know what to look for with leaks. You usually won't know if the valve is inoperative, since we recommend you not try them.

Rust or Damage

CAUSES

Rust on valves is usually caused by leaks. Rust may make the valve inoperative and may cause further leakage.

Valves can be mechanically damaged. Handles are commonly broken and stems can be bent.

STRATEGY

Advise your client to ask the service person to operate all valves during regular servicing. Recommend that any obviously damaged valves be repaired or replaced.

CHAPTER REVIEW QUESTIONS

Answer the following questions on a separate sheet of paper, then check your results against the answers provided in Appendix E. If you have trouble with a question, refer back to the chapter to review the relevant material.

1. List the four safety controls found on all hydronic systems.
2. What is the normal operating pressure in a boiler?
   a. 2 to 5 psi
   b. 5 to 9 psi
   c. 9 to 12 psi
   d. 12 to 15 psi
   e. 15 to 18 psi

3. What is the normal setting on the pressure-relief valve?

    a. 10 psi

    b. 20 psi

    c. 30 psi

    d. 40 psi

    e. 50 psi

4. Where is the pressure-relief valve typically located? Also, where does it typically discharge?

5. Are we required to test the pressure-relief valve?

    Yes   No

6. Is it possible to have a pressure-relief valve that is too small for the boiler?

    Yes   No

7. What is common temperature setting for the high-temperature limit switch?

    a. 180°F

    b. 195°F

    c. 210°F

    d. 225°F

    e. 240°F

8. What is the purpose of the low-water cutout on a large residential boiler?

9. Why do we need a backflow preventer on a modern hydronic system?

10. What is the safety control that prevents us from getting superheated water in a boiler system?

    a. The circulator

    b. The pressure-relief valve

    c. The backflow preventer

    d. The pressure-reducing valve

    e. The heat exchanger

11. List six operating controls that we may find on a hydronic system.

12. What is the function of the pressure-reducing valve?

13. In a two-story Victorian home with a boiler in the basement you find a pressure-reducing valve set to 12 psi. Is there a possibility that this valve is set too low?

    Yes   No

14. Is it possible for a boiler to function without a pressure-reducing valve?

    Yes   No

15. What is the purpose of an automatic air vent on a boiler? Are they mandatory?

16. You find a boiler with a low-temperature limit or primary control. What would be a typical setting for this control?

    a. 50°F

    b. 100°F

    c. 140°F

    d. 180°F

    e. 220°F

17. List three ways that the system can control a circulator (pump).

18. What is the purpose of zone control in larger houses?

KEY TERMS

pressure-relief valve	backflow preventer	outdoor-air thermostat
high-temperature limit switch	pressure reducing valve	primary control
	zone control	flow control valve
low-water cutout	air vent	pump control

3

DISTRIBUTION SYSTEMS

LEARNING OBJECTIVES

At the end of this chapter you should be able to:

- list four problems found with expansion tanks
- list three problems found with pumps
- list four problems found with pipes

3.1 OVERVIEW

Move the Heat

The function of the hot water distribution system is the same as the function of the warm air distribution system with furnaces. We are trying to get the heat from the boiler to the rooms we want to heat.

There are four basic components to the distribution system—

1. Pump (circulator)
2. Pipes
3. Radiators, convectors, or baseboards
4. Expansion tank

We'll look at each of these components more closely later in this section.

Pumps are traditionally brass, bronze, and steel. Piping is traditionally black steel with cast-iron fittings. It may also be copper. In modern systems, plastics such as polybutylene and cross-linked polyethylene are used.

Radiators are traditionally cast iron. Convectors can be cast iron, steel, or copper. Baseboards may be cast iron, steel, copper, aluminum, or a combination of these.

Expansion tanks are typically galvanized steel.

Most modern systems are closed. Some older open systems are still in service. There is not a great difference between how the two systems work, but you should be able to identify a couple of things.

3.1.1 Open System

High Expansion Tank with Overflow

The **open expansion tank** system is typically a loop using **pipes** and radiators (Figure 3.1). The system has an expansion tank located at the top of the home above the highest radiator. An overflow pipe, leading out from this expansion tank, is open to the atmosphere. The pipe may extend out through the roof or wall of the building, discharging outside. It may also discharge inside the building into a drainage system.

Function

The expansion tank on an open system allows the water to expand as it heats up. The purpose of putting the expansion tank at the top of the system is to allow the system to be filled, to be able to check the water level, and to create a significant pressure (head) at the boiler, allowing the water to heat up more without getting close to boiling. The greater the pressure there is on water, the more difficult it is for water to boil. Remember, although we call them boilers, we don't want the water to boil in hot water heating systems.

No Pump or Relief Valve

Open systems do not have a **circulator (pump)** and they do not have a pressure-relief valve in the system. The opening to atmosphere is adequate pressure relief.

Open systems don't have a pump control or a primary control. Open systems have manual water makeup. There is no pressure-reducing valve and usually no backflow preventer.

Providing Water Makeup

Open systems have a manual valve that can be used to add water to the system. The expansion tanks typically have sight glasses that show how much water is in the tanks. When the water falls below the level of the sight glass, water can be added manually. The valves are sometimes located beside the expansion tank at the top of the home. In other systems, the water make-up valve is located close to   the

Overfilling

boiler. Overfilling the system is not a huge problem, since excess water can discharge through the overflow pipe to the outdoors or a safe drain location.

F I G U R E 3.1   Open Hydronic System

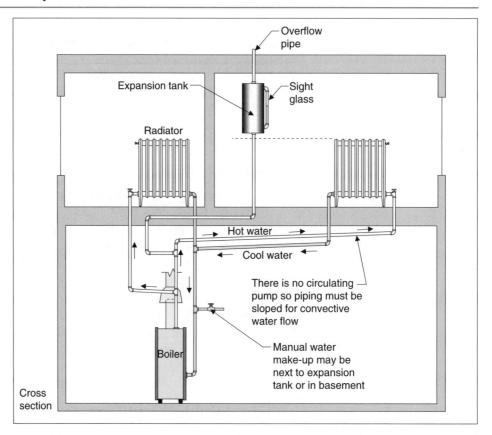

3.1.2 Closed System

Pump and Pressure Relief

The modern closed hot water system has the expansion tank just above the boiler, usually at ceiling level (Figure 3.2). It has eliminated the open discharge to the atmosphere and has added a (circulator) pump. A pressure-relief valve (set at 30 psi) is needed since the system now could overpressurize itself if the burner failed to shut off.

Better Heating

The closed system improves operation and allows for the forced circulating system. The house is more evenly heated. Zone control is possible (and effective) on closed systems.

Don't Need a Pump

There are a few closed systems that do not have a pump. This is not a mistake, but the pumps do add comfort and some efficiency.

Pressure-Reducing Valve

Modern closed systems typically have an automatic water makeup system using a pressure-reducing valve. This is simply a more convenient approach. It automatically adds water to the system as it is needed.

Backflow Preventer

Closed systems often (but not always) have backflow preventers. If you see an expansion tank just above the boiler, a pressure-relief valve, a pressure-reducing valve, and a circulating pump, you know for sure you have a closed system. This is what you'll see most of the time.

3.1.3 Types of Piping Systems

There are three basic types of piping systems:

1. The series loop
2. One-pipe system
3. Two-pipe system

FIGURE 3.2 Closed Hydronic System

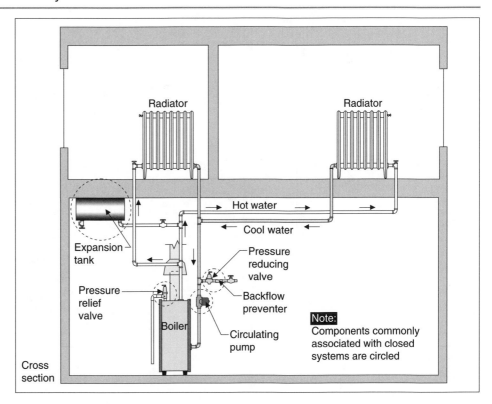

Series Loop

The series loop is the simplest and least expensive hot water piping arrangement (Figure 3.3). The water that leaves the boiler flows in a simple loop throughout the system. All of the water flows through each radiator or convector in series.

Crude

The disadvantage of this system is that the first radiator sees the hottest water, the second radiator sees the second hottest water, etc. The last radiator may see water that is quite cool. The heating system is likely to be somewhat uneven.

One-Pipe System

The one-pipe system is slightly more sophisticated (Figure 3.4). One main pipe forms a loop around the house. At each radiator, some of the water is diverted to the radiator. The water that flows through the radiator is dumped back into the main pipe. Some of the water carries on past each radiator and some is diverted through the radiator, before rejoining the main pipe. The radiators will see slightly more even temperatures, although, again, the further you go down the loop, the cooler the water is going to be.

Two-Pipe System

The two-pipe system is one step more sophisticated (Figure 3.5). Two pipes go from the boiler throughout the house. The supply pipe carries hot water from the boiler. At each radiator, there is a takeoff from the supply pipe to the radiator. After the water flows through the radiator and is cooled, it is connected to a return pipe. At each radiator, water is fed from the hot pipe into the radiator. The cold water from the radiator is dumped into the return pipe. This is a more even type of heating system.

Direct Return and Reverse Return

The return loop can be simple or complicated. In a direct return system, the cold water from each radiator flows directly back to the boiler to be reheated. In a reverse return system, the return water flows out to the end of the loop before returning to the boiler in a straight, uninterrupted run (Figure 3.6).

F I G U R E 3.3 Series Loop

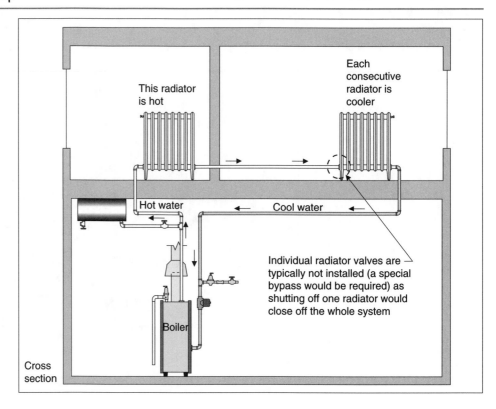

F I G U R E 3.4 One-Pipe System

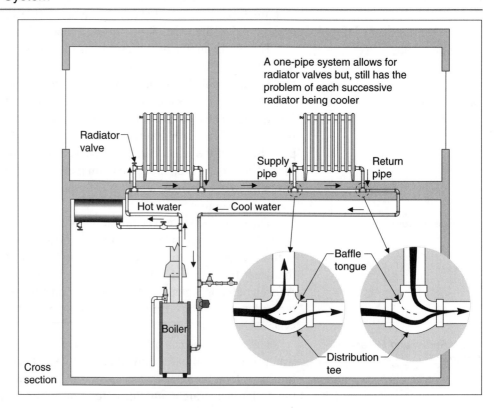

F I G U R E 3.5   Two-Pipe System (Direct Return)

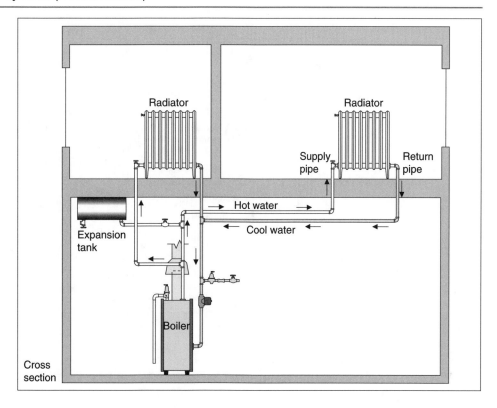

F I G U R E 3.6   Two-Pipe System (Reverse Return)

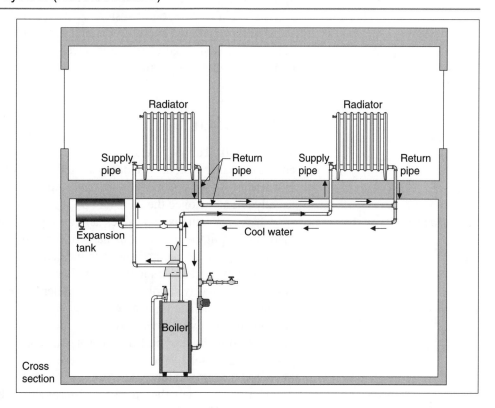

F I G U R E 3.7   Balancing Methods

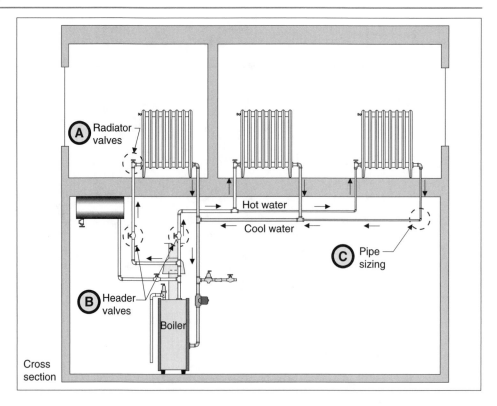

The reverse return system yields a slightly more even heat than the direct return system. The distance that the water has to flow is similar for every radiator in the system with a reverse return system.

What We Say

As inspectors, we should recognize the different systems and understand the comparative advantages. We would never tell someone to rip out any of these systems, unless there were other considerations.

3.1.4   Balancing

When we talked about furnaces, we found that there were a number of ways to balance the heating system with dampers in the ducts and at the registers (Figure 3.7). Hot water heating systems can be balanced as well, although in practice they are usually left alone once they are set up.

At the Header

There are often manual valves at main supply headers near the boiler, where the main feeds split to go to various parts of the house.

Pipe Sizing

The original balancing is done in the layout and sizing of the supply and return pipes. The pipe diameters may get smaller as we go further down the system. This is similar to the way supply ducts get smaller as we move further from the furnace.

Radiator Valves

Individual balancing can be done at each radiator. Most radiators have manually operated valves. There are some thermostatically operated valves that are designed to modulate the flow of water through the radiator based on a desired temperature chosen by the occupant. These valves have a dial or gauge allowing you to choose the temperature you want.

Control Flow Through Radiators

These valves, whether manual or thermostatic, control the water flow through the radiator. Whenever the pump is working, water will flow through each radiator. Adjusting these valves adjusts the amount of water that flows. If the valve is completely shut off, there will still be water in the radiator and it will still be directly connected to the return side. However, no water will flow through the radiator, and the water in the radiator itself will remain cold, since it isn't circulated past the boiler on a regular basis.

Not on a Series System!

The balancing valves we've been talking about cannot be used on a series loop. If we closed off a valve going into a radiator on a series loop, no water would flow. None of the radiators would get any heat if one radiator valve was closed. This is one clue to identifying a series loop system. There will be no valves on the radiators.

3.2   EXPANSION TANKS

The function of the expansion tank is somewhat incidental to the whole distribution system. However, we're going to be referring to them a number of times, so we may as well deal with them now.

The expansion tank allows the water to expand as it heats up, without dramatically increasing the system pressure. Water, like many other materials, wants to expand when it's heated. If we didn't have an expansion tank in the system, the water pressure would increase dramatically when the boiler came on. This can cause stress on components, make the water more difficult to circulate, and may lead to superheated water and steam explosions.

Shock Absorber

The expansion tank is an air cushion or shock absorber. The tank is partially filled with water from the boiler system. The top part of the tank is filled with trapped air.

Water Level Changes in the Tank

If the tank is one-third filled with water when the boiler is cold, the water level will rise when the boiler fires (Figure 3.8). Air is quite compressible and can be readily squeezed without increasing pressure dramatically. It acts like an easily

FIGURE 3.8   Expansion Tank Water Levels

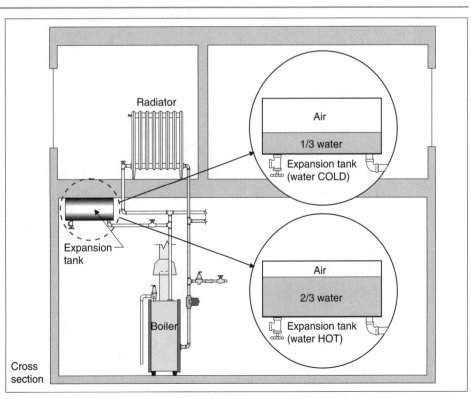

compressed spring. When the boiler is operating at steady state, the expansion tank may be two-thirds filled with water.

Material   Expansion tanks are typically galvanized steel. The older tanks were very often unpainted. Modern tanks are usually prepainted at the factory.

3.2.1   Location and Type

Open-System Tanks   In homes with open hot water systems, the expansion tanks would be located on the top floor, often in a closet. The bottom of the tank would be above the top of the highest radiator. These tanks could be cylindrical, rectangular, or other shapes. They often had a sight glass so that you could see the level of water in the tank.

Overflow Pipe   There was always an overflow tube coming off the top of the tank, usually made of galvanized steel (Figure 3.9). There was sometimes a water makeup valve and pipe connected to the expansion tank so that water could be added from the supply plumbing pipes. The water from the heating system was, of course, always connected to the tank, at the bottom.

Closed-System Tanks   On closed systems, there are two types of expansion tanks:

1. Conventional
2. Diaphragm or bladder tank

Tank Differences   The conventional tank is just a metal cylinder. The **diaphragm expansion tank** has a loose rubber bladder separating the tank into two compartments. One is the air side, and the other is the water side, which is connected to the boiler through a pipe.

FIGURE 3.9   Overflow Pipe

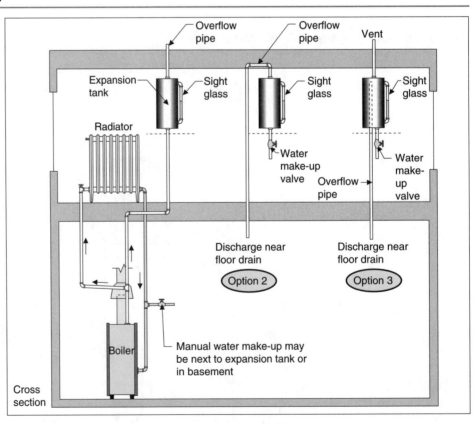

F I G U R E 3.10 Conventional Expansion Tank

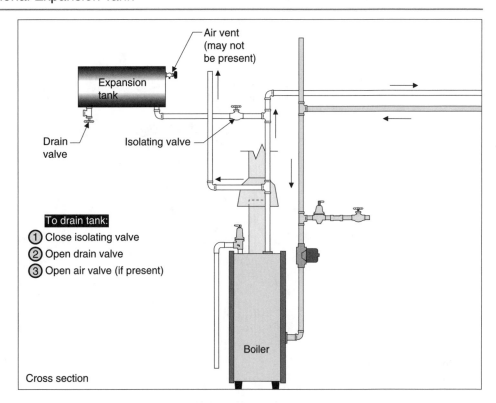

Cross section

Conventional Tank

On closed systems, it's common to find the expansion tank strapped between ceiling joists above the boiler. If the ceiling is plastered, the tank may be barely visible. These tanks are typically cylinders, 8 to 10 inches in diameter and 18 inches to 3 feet long installed horizontally.

Pipe Connections

They typically have one pipe connected to the heating system, usually tapped into the hot water distribution supply pipe coming off the boiler. The expansion tank has a drain valve and may have an air inlet valve that can be opened to allow air into the tank as the water is drained out (Figure 3.10).

Isolating Valve

The piping between the heating system and the expansion tank usually has an isolating valve that can be manually closed to allow the tank to be drained.

Air Bubbles Collected

Air can be eliminated from the top of a boiler with an air scoop or separator, and the bubbles will rise into the tank.

Diaphragm Tanks

Conventional tanks have to be mounted above the boiler. Diaphragm tanks can be anywhere, including above or below the top of the boiler. Tanks can be on the supply or return side of the boiler. Boilers with diaphragm tanks usually have an air vent.

Bicycle Valve on Diaphragm Tanks

The air side of the diaphragm tank usually has a "bicycle tire"–style valve that can be used to pressurize the air side of the tank (Figure 3.11). If you operate this valve and get water, it means the bladder has ruptured. This is not a test required by the standards or recommended by us.

3.2.2 Operation

Setting Up the System with a Conventional Tank

When the heating system is first set up, all the pipes are filled with air. The expansion tank is completely filled with air as well. You can think of the expansion tank as a large dead-end part of the heating system. When water

FIGURE 3.11   Diaphragm Tank

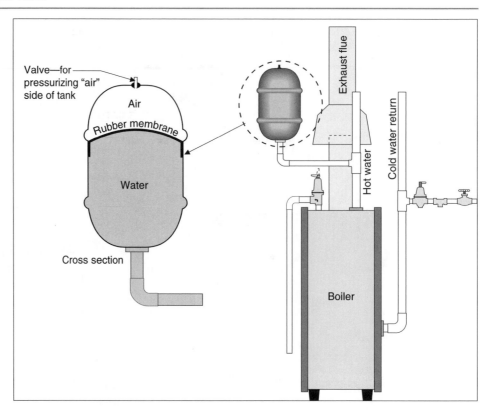

is introduced, the pipes will be filled with water, but air will be trapped in the expansion tank. This is what we want. The expansion tank typically has some water that comes into the bottom of it, but the majority of its volume remains filled with air.

Normal Operation

As the boiler operates, the air in the tank is compressed and the tank may be more than half filled with water when the system is hot.

Air Dissolved over Time

The air eventually is lost from the conventional expansion tank. It sometimes leaks out slowly through the air valve, but the majority is dissolved into the water over time.

Waterlogged Tank

When the tank is filled with water, it is said to be waterlogged. The system loses its shock absorber. When the boiler comes on, the pressure in the system will rise quickly. If all goes well, the relief valve operates and water leaks out through the discharge pipe from the relief valve. If the relief valve is missing, inoperative, or its discharge is obstructed, a dangerous high-pressure situation can develop.

Restoring the System

The homeowner or service person will notice the relief valve discharging and eventually will notice that the expansion tank is waterlogged. Restoring the air in the tank is done as follows:

1. The isolating valve on the pipe connecting the heating system to the expansion tank is closed.

2. A hose is usually connected to the fitting on the drain valve, and the drain valve is opened.

3. The air inlet valve (usually located near the top of the tank) is also opened.

4. The water runs out of the drain line and air is introduced through the air inlet.

5. When the tank is empty—

   a. the hose is removed from the fitting,

   b. the drain valve is closed,

   c. the air inlet is closed, and

   d. the isolating valve is opened.

6. Water from the heating system makes its way up into the bottom of the tank, compressing the air.

7. The system is ready for operation again.

A Modern Improvement

Many modern expansion tanks have a rubber (neoprene) diaphragm that separates the air and the water, as discussed. The system works exactly the same, but the flexible rubber diaphragm keeps the air from being dissolved into the water. These systems rarely become waterlogged and are therefore more convenient.

Where Is the Best Spot for the Expansion Tank?

There is some controversy about where the expansion tank is best located. However, for the purposes of a home inspection, as long as it is present and connected to the heating system, we don't have to worry. In most cases, you'll see it on the hot water supply distribution pipe coming off the top of the boiler. (Conventional tanks on closed systems have to be above the top of the boiler.) If the tank is connected to the return side of the boiler, the system will still work just fine, maybe better.

3.2.3   Conditions

Expansion tanks are subject to any of the following problems:

1. Leaks
2. Waterlogged
3. Rust
4. Too small
5. Poor discharge location for open tank
6. Poor location for tank

Leaks

CAUSES

Tanks may leak because of poor connections, rust, or mechanical damage.

IMPLICATIONS

The implications of leakage are water damage and possible overheating of the boiler, if other controls do not work properly.

STRATEGY

Check for leaks at the expansion tank, drain valve, isolating valve, and air inlet.

Waterlogged

CAUSE

When the air is dissolved into the water of the heating system, the expansion tank may become waterlogged.

IMPLICATIONS

Pressure in the system will rise quickly when the boiler operates. The relief valve should operate. If it does not, the system may become overpressurized, creating an unsafe condition.

STRATEGY

When the boiler operates, watch the pressure gauge on the boiler. It should move from about 12 to 15 psi when the boiler is cool, up to a maximum of 25 psi. It may not even get above 15 psi. If the gauge gets close to 30 psi and/or the relief valve operates, the expansion tank may be waterlogged. Recommend that this be checked by a service person.

Rust

Rust is caused by—

CAUSE

- humidity and/or condensation in the environment.
- old age
- long-term exposure to water and air inside the tank
- harsh chemicals being used nearby
- poor quality unit or manufacturer's defect

IMPLICATION

A rusted tank is prone to leakage.

STRATEGY

Look at the tank and its fittings for evidence of rust.

Too Small

This is an installation issue.

CAUSE

IMPLICATIONS

The implications of an undersized tank are pressure build-up in the system and discharge of the relief valve.

STRATEGY

We've talked about looking for pressure build-up and discharge of the relief valve. It is usually the result of a waterlogged tank. On new installations, it can be the result of an undersized expansion tank. This is more likely to occur on large homes where the volume of water in the system is considerable.

Poor Discharge Location for Open Tank

This may be an installation or remodeling issue.

CAUSE

IMPLICATION

Water damage to the house is the implication.

STRATEGY

Follow the overflow pipe from the expansion tank on the highest floor, to its end. Where does the water go? It should go outside or into a drain. We find many that end in the attic.

Where you find a poor discharge spot, look for water damage, including rot. Sometimes that intermittent "roof leak" turns out to be an overflow pipe problem!

Poor Location for Tank

The proper location for an expansion tank depends on the system.

CAUSES

1. Open tanks should be above the highest radiators. If the attic is finished as part of a renovation, the tank may end up below some new radiators.
2. Closed system conventional tanks should be above the boiler. Where they are beside the boiler, it's an installation problem.

IMPLICATIONS

The implications are—

1. Inadequate heat for the upper radiators on open tanks.
2. Air getting into the boiler from the expansion tank on a closed system.

STRATEGY

Watch for these location problems. Remember that diaphragm tanks can be beside the boiler, but conventional tanks can't.

3.3   PUMPS OR CIRCULATORS

Function

The pump (circulator) on a hot water heating system has the same function as the fan on a forced-air heating system. We are pushing the heat transfer medium (water) from the boiler out to the rooms we want to heat.

Works on Return and Supply

Just like the fan on a forced-air system, the pump pushes the heated water out to the system and pulls the cool water back. The pump does not create large pressures and is relatively small. The pump motor is often $1/12$ horsepower. It works more like a paddle wheel moving the water slowly through the system than a fire pump trying to build up pressure.

Location

The pump is typically located on the return piping adjacent to the boiler. Some feel that the pumps work better if they pump away from the boiler. This means putting the pump on the supply piping. Either location is acceptable.

Not Too High or Low

Pumps are usually beside the boiler. They shouldn't be at a low point in the piping because sediment collects here. They shouldn't be at a high point because air bubbles collect here. Air in a pump can damage it.

Electric Motor Driven

The pump is driven by an electric motor and there is often a mechanical coupling between the motor and the pump (Figure 3.12). The pump is an impeller type and does not shut off the flow of water when the pump is idle.

Water Flows Past Idle Pump

If the pump does not operate, some flow of water can be expected through the system by convection.

Pump Orientation

The motor should be beside the pump rather than above or below it. The shaft of the motor and pump are designed to be horizontal. If the shaft is vertical, the bearings will fail quickly.

Pumps Need Lubrication

Conventional pumps require lubrication. The electric motor typically has two lubrication ports and the coupler has one.

FIGURE 3.12   Circulating Pump

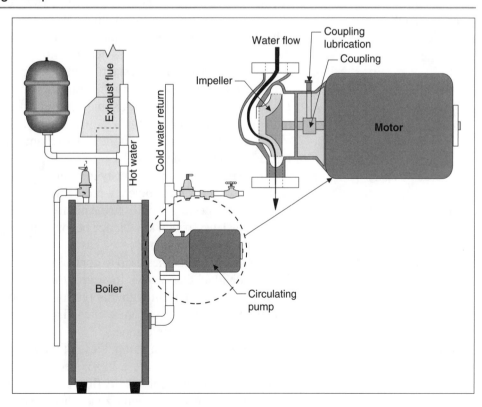

These pumps have been around since the 1930s. Their performance is excellent as long as they are lubricated. If neglected, of course, they will seize.

Another Type of Pump

A more modern and less expensive pump is a permanently lubricated pump and motor. The sealed bearings (actually bushings) in the coupler and motor do not require regular maintenance. However, some maintain that their life is shorter than the older type.

A Third Type of Pump

Some pumps are water lubricated. The pump and motor are integral in one housing. The water in the heating system lubricates the assembly. The motor is sealed so that it can be immersed in the water. These are common on new systems because they are maintenance free and inexpensive. Many modern package boilers are sold with an integral pump, sized correctly for the boiler.

Operating Controls

The pump may be activated by—

1. The thermostat
2. Electric power being on to the boiler (in this case, the pump runs continuously through the heating season)
3. Pump control (aquastat) that senses the water temperature leaving the boiler

In the Controls section, we talked about the various ways that pumps could be activated. It depends on the philosophy of the system designer and, to a certain extent, the type of boiler.

Copper Boilers Need Pump on

We have said that copper-tube boilers have to have the pump operating before the burner can come on safely. These very thin heat exchangers need a constant supply of cold water to keep them from overheating.

Boiler Condensation a Possibility

Many people feel that the best type of pump control is having the pump come on only when the boiler is up to temperature. (This only applies if the heat exchanger can take the heat without water moving through it.) They feel this will minimize condensation in the boiler. When a boiler is warming up, the exhaust gases are exposed to a cold heat exchanger and cold water on the other side. The exhaust gases may cool to their dew point (about 125°F) before they escape up through the chimney.

Leave Pump Off While Boiler Heats?

Turning the pump on and cycling cold water through the heat exchanger makes it harder for the boiler to heat up and increases the risk of condensation. Leaving the water in the boiler while it's heating should help reduce condensation.

Systems that use an aquastat to control the pump usually do not have the pump come on until the boiler water temperature is 110°F to 140°F.

Another Advantage

When the boiler shuts off, some pumps shut off immediately. This leaves heat in the heat exchanger that finds its way up the chimney. It's more energy-efficient to keep the pump running until the heat exchanger has cooled. We may as well capture as much of the heat as we can.

Continuous Pumping

If the pump runs continuously throughout the heating season, the condensation problem exists but the efficiency problem on shutdown does not.

The Inspector's Role

Home inspectors would never advise clients to rearrange the pump set-up, unless they have special knowledge beyond the scope of a home inspection. Again, we are not system designers.

Pumps Used for Zone Control

Pumps are sometimes used to control various zones in heating systems (Figure 3.13). Individual thermostats for various parts of the house can activate their own pumps to move water through that part of the house. Where zone valves are used, one of several zone valves can be opened and the main pump can be activated at the same time to heat a single zone.

Flow Control Valves

We said earlier that a pump does not provide a positive shutoff to water movement when the pump is at rest. In a zoned system, this can lead to overheating of a zone that's not calling for heat. A flow control valve is often put into the system to prevent water flowing through a zone when the pump is off (Figure 3.14). When the

FIGURE 3.13   Zone Control with Pumps

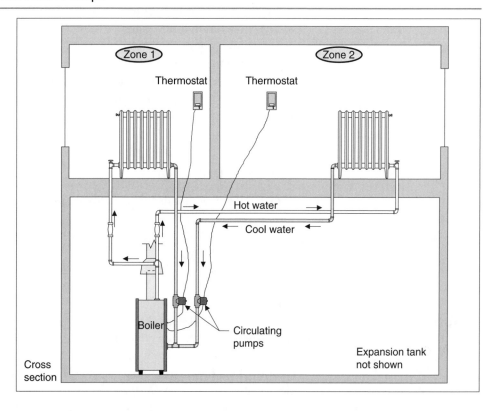

FIGURE 3.14   Flow Control Valve

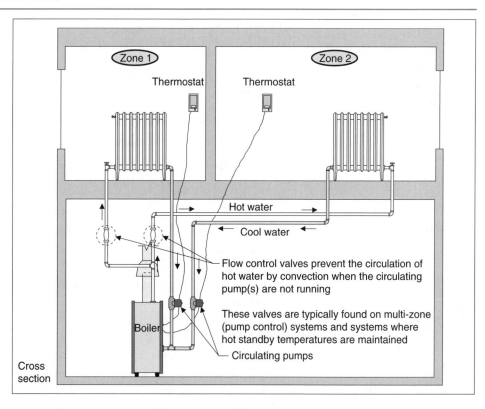

pump is activated, there is enough force to open the flow control valve. When the pump shuts off, the flow control valve closes and there will be no gravity or convective flow through that zone.

Reverse Flow Protection

The flow control valve also prevents reverse flow through an idle branch, which is possible on some systems, when another zone is working.

Boiler Kept Hot

The flow control valve is also often used whenever the boiler is kept hot on standby, even if there is only one zone. Without it, the system would operate as a gravity (convective) system when there is no call for heat. The house may overheat.

3.3.1 Conditions

Look for these problems when checking pumps:

1. Leaks
2. Inoperative
3. Noisy or hot

Leaks

CAUSE

Pumps have several stages of seals inside to maintain the water seal at the pump shaft. Over time, these seals may wear out.

IMPLICATIONS

The implications are water damage, poor heat circulation, and possible overheating of the boiler. There may be an electrical problem as well if the leak is onto electric controls for the pump or the motor itself.

STRATEGY

Look for evidence of leakage at the pump. Very often there is lubricating oil on and below the pump. Don't mistake this for water leakage.

Watch It Run

Make sure you look at the pump when it is operating.

Inoperative

When the boiler is running and up to temperature, the pump should be working, unless there is more than one pump. In a zoned system with multiple pumps, only the pump for the zone needing heat will run.

CAUSES

An inoperative pump may result from several causes:

■ there may be an electrical problem with the motor
■ the motor itself may be seized or burned out
■ the pump bearings may have seized
■ the coupler may have failed
■ the pump controls may also be set up improperly or may be defective

IMPLICATIONS

An inoperative pump will make the house less comfortable, increase the heating costs, and may overheat the heat exchanger. Some heat exchangers are very susceptible to damage if the burner fires when the pump is not working. If the pump is interlocked with the burner (copper-tube boiler) there will be no heat if the pump doesn't work.

STRATEGY

Make sure the pump operates when the heating system is running. Don't try to troubleshoot pumps that don't come on.

Noisy or Hot

CAUSES

If the pump is very noisy or hot to the touch when running, service should be recommended. Bearing problems are the most common difficulty. The noise may also be the impeller hitting the housing.

The implications of a noisy or overheated pump are, at the very least, repairs and possibly replacement of the pump or coupler.

Squeals, whining, grinding noises, and chatter are indications that the pump and/or motor is in distress.

Look for an air vent. These help pumps by eliminating air, which can damage pumps.

Practice touching pumps and motor casings (be careful!) to get a sense of the normal operating temperature. You should not be burned on contact. The water-lubricated pumps will run cooler. They should be at the return water temperature. The air-cooled, conventional electric motor attached to the pump through a coupler should run at the same temperature as any electric motor (hot to the touch).

3.4   PIPES

Function

The distribution piping system carries the water from the boiler to the radiator, convector, or baseboard. In a radiant system, the piping is also the final distribution mechanism.

Material

The piping on older systems is black steel. The fittings may be steel or cast iron. Copper piping is also used. Some modern systems use plastic piping, including polybutylene and cross-linked polyethylene.

Doesn't the Steel Piping Rust?

When we talk about the plumbing system, we'll find that the galvanized steel supply plumbing pipes rust after 40 to 60 years of service. You might think that the black steel piping used in heating systems would rust even faster since it doesn't have the benefit of galvanizing. Actually, the heating pipes last a good deal longer than the plumbing pipes. There is a good reason for this.

Fresh Water Worse than Stale Water

Plumbing pipes are always exposed to fresh water flowing through them. The water is not recycled in a supply plumbing system (we hope). On a heating system, the same water is recycled many, many times. The water should not be changed even over a period of years if possible.

Lack of Oxygen

The fresh water the plumbing pipes continually see brings with it a fresh supply of oxygen and opportunity for corrosion. The boiler water is effectively inert and contains very little oxygen once it's been in place for some time. That's why we get away with black steel piping on hot water heating systems. It often lasts 70 to 90 years.

Location

The piping is run throughout the house and is mostly concealed. Even where it might be exposed in basements or crawl spaces, it is often insulated to keep the heat inside the piping until it gets to the radiators.

Reliable

For the most part, the piping is not a troublesome part of the hot water heating system.

3.4.1   Conditions

Look for the following pipe problems:

1. Rust
2. Leaks
3. Crimped
4. Too small
5. Poor support
6. No insulation

F I G U R E 3.15   Pipe Corrosion

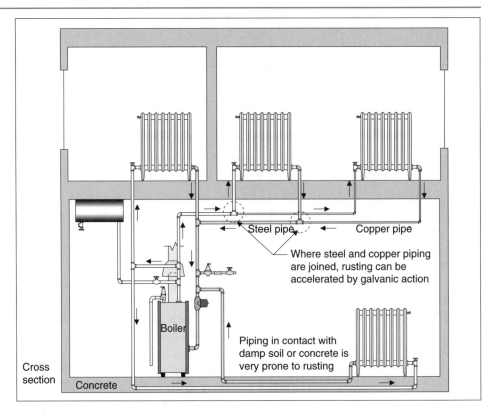

Rust

Most piping will rust eventually. However, the black steel piping can last a very long time and copper piping can last almost indefinitely.

CAUSES

Rust is a natural process with metals exposed to oxygen and water. It takes place very slowly; however, a couple of things can accelerate the rusting process dramatically.

Dissimilar Metals

When a steel piping system is extended with copper piping, the possibility of a galvanic reaction is established (Figure 3.15). The dissimilar metals tend to create an accelerated rusting process and the steel is often sacrificed.

Piping in the Soil

Piping in contact with damp soil can lead to fast rusting . This is true of steel and copper piping. Certain soil types are quite corrosive.

IMPLICATIONS

The implications of rusted pipes are leaking and clogging. Both can lead to inefficiencies, water damage, and a no-heat condition.

STRATEGY

Look for evidence of rusting, especially where dissimilar metals join and where pipes are in contact with soil. Also look at connections. Wherever threads have to be cut into pipes, the pipe wall is thinner. Rust may show up first here.

In some cases, rusting can scab over and stop a leak temporarily. If you see evidence of rusting, but no water, there may be an intermittent leak that is going to get worse.

Leaks

CAUSES

Pipes may leak because of rust, mechanical damage, poor connections, or freezing.

IMPLICATIONS

Water damage, a loss of efficiency, and a no-heat condition are all possible implications of leaks.

FIGURE 3.16 Extending Hot Water Systems

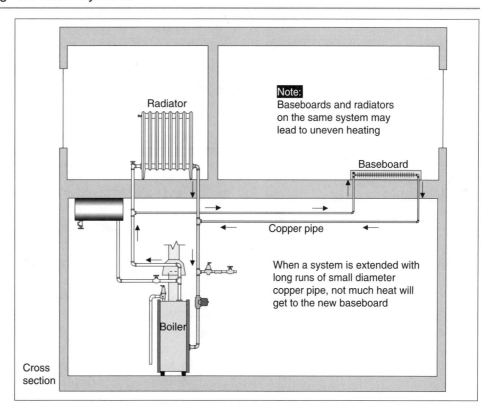

Radiator

Note:
Baseboards and radiators
on the same system may
lead to uneven heating

Baseboard

Copper pipe

When a system is extended with
long runs of small diameter
copper pipe, not much heat will
get to the new baseboard

Boiler

Cross
section

Look at as much of the visible piping as possible, focusing on connections. One of the most common leakage spots on hot water heating systems is where the piping connects to the radiator. The radiator valves are frequently sources of leaks.

Crimped

This is more of an issue with copper and plastic piping than steel.

Crimping is caused by mechanical damage either during or after installation.

The implications of crimping are reduced flow, reduced comfort, and higher heating costs.

Look for crimping along any exposed pipe lengths.

Too Small

Undersized piping is usually the result of heating systems being extended by someone other than the original installer. This is often done when houses have additions. Incidentally, this is the time when dissimilar materials are most likely to be used on a distribution piping system.

Systems Extended

We have seen many systems where large-diameter steel pipes have been extended with small-diameter copper pipes running several feet to a new baseboard, far away from the boiler (Figure 3.16). It should not be a surprise that the baseboard will not deliver much heat.

The implication of undersized piping is inadequate heating.

Where you see systems extended with pipes that are much smaller than the rest of the distribution system, raise the possibility of a poor comfort condition. You probably won't be able to be conclusive, but you can suggest that people either try it and see for themselves, or have a service person look at the condition.

Poor Support

Steel heating pipes are typically supported every 10 feet horizontally. Heavy metal straps or hangers are used. Copper pipe should be supported about every 7 feet, depending on its diameter. Copper or plastic (not steel) hangers should be used.

CAUSE

Poor support on an old system is usually the result of modifications.

IMPLICATION

Poor support can result in leaks.

STRATEGY

Look for supports and for sagging pipes.

No Insulation

This is an installation or renovation problem.

CAUSES

There may be no implications. Many pipes are not insulated, but everything works well. However, a lack of insulation can mean overheating, particularly in rooms close to the boiler, or too much heat loss before the water gets to the radiators, which makes rooms cool.

IMPLICATIONS

STRATEGY

Look for long runs of uninsulated pipes. In the heating season, you'll be able to identify the hot and cold parts of the house. In the summer, you'll be guessing.

Watch for pipes running through unheated spots, crawl spaces, garages, etc. These pipes should be insulated.

May Contain Asbestos

Some insulation on boilers and pipes contains asbestos. This is an environmental issue in some areas. It's beyond our scope. You can't tell if the insulation contains asbestos by looking.

Do not Disturb

Our advice is, don't disturb the insulation. We tell our clients that we don't deal with environmental issues such as asbestos, lead, radon, UFFI (urea formaldehyde foam insulation), etc. Many inspectors do. If you choose to address these issues, we suggest you get some good knowledge first.

CHAPTER REVIEW QUESTIONS

Answer the following questions on a separate sheet of paper, then check your results against the answers provided in Appendix E. If you have trouble with a question, refer back to the chapter to review the relevant material.

1. What are the four components in the distribution system for a hot water system?
2. What is the basic difference between an open system and a closed system?
3. Where is the expansion tank, typically, in an open system?
4. What is the purpose of the reverse return in a two-pipe closed system?
5. Closed systems must have circulators.

   True   False
6. What is the function of the expansion tank in a closed water system?
7. Where is the expansion tank, typically, in a closed hot water system?
8. List three styles of circulators.
9. List three materials that have been used for distribution piping in hot water systems in the past.

10. When a black steel pipe is extended with copper pipe, what can occur?

    a. The steel pipe may rust at the connection due to galvanic reaction.

    b. The circulator may not be able to overcome the pressure change at the junction.

    c. The copper pipe will wear through with the friction force of the water.

    d. The copper pipe will rust because of the galvanic reaction.

    e. Nothing occurs when steel and copper piping are joined.

11. In a radiant hot water heating system, the pipes serve two purposes. What are they?

KEY TERMS

open expansion tank	bladder (diaphragm)	circulator (pump)
closed expansion tank	expansion tank	pipes

CHAPTER

4

RADIATORS, CONVECTORS, AND BASEBOARDS

LEARNING OBJECTIVES

At the end of this chapter you should be able to:

■ list and describe the four styles of heat delivery that are used with boilers

■ list the eight problems found with radiators, convectors, and baseboards

F I G U R E 4.1   Covering Radiators Reduces Efficiency

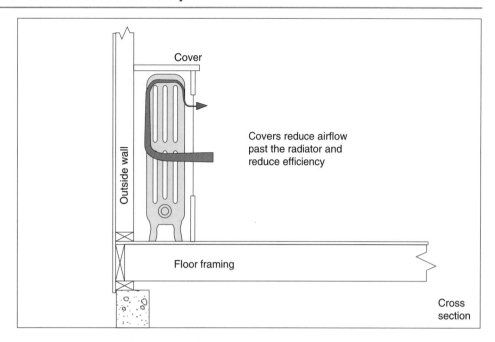

4.1 OVERVIEW

Radiators

Convectors

Another Definition

Baseboards

Radiators, convectors, and baseboards have the same function as the registers on supply ducts in forced air systems. This part of the distribution system releases the heat into the room.

Radiators are usually cast iron. They can stand on feet, hang on walls, or hang from ceilings. Some old radiators were quite decorative; more modern radiators are fairly plain. Radiators are designed to be freestanding, although many people put wooden enclosures around them to make them look better. This does reduce their efficiency to some extent, although it doesn't make them useless (Figure 4.1).

Depending on what part of North America you're from, **convectors** can mean slightly different things. To many, convectors mean the next step in the evolution of heating systems after radiators. Convectors are typically cast iron enclosed in a sheet metal cabinet with openings at the bottom and near the top (Figure 4.2). They do not radiate heat as directly as radiators because the hot surface of the cast iron is enclosed by the sheet metal. They do a majority of their heating by convection, drawing cool air at the bottom and expelling the heated air from the top.

If radiators heat 50 percent by convection and 50 percent by radiation, convectors heat 70 percent to 90 percent by convection and only 10 percent to 30 percent by radiation.

Other people think of convectors as the low-profile systems that look like baseboard heaters.

Other people refer to the very-low-profile systems as **baseboard** heating. In some areas, baseboard heating only means electric baseboard. In other areas, baseboard heating can mean hot water, electric, or steam. With respect to hot water, baseboards are low profile, often projecting only 3 inches out from a wall surface. They are typically 10 inches tall or less and are encased in a metal cabinet. Again, they have openings at the bottom to introduce cool air, and openings at the top to allow warm air into the room (Figure 4.3).

F I G U R E 4.2 Convector

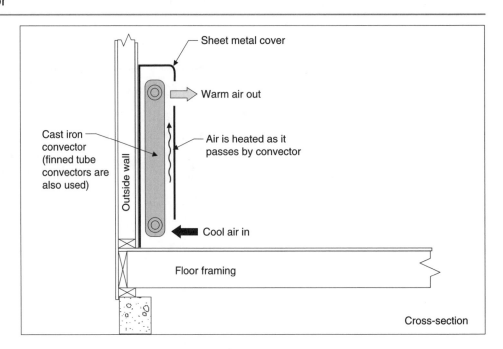

Cross-section

F I G U R E 4.3 Cast-Iron Baseboard

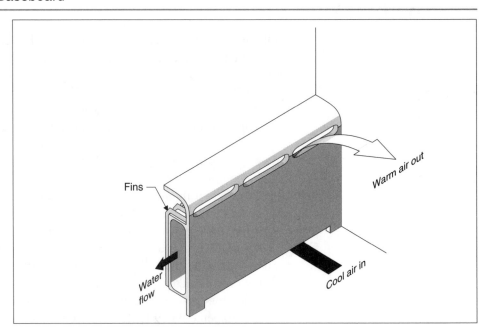

The Guts of a Baseboard   Baseboards can be cast iron, steel, copper, aluminum, or a combination of these. Copper tubes with aluminum fins are common convector materials. Steel tubes with steel fins are also common (Figure 4.4).

Relative Capacities   Radiators are tall and quite bulky. They have more heat capacity per length than convectors, baseboards, and radiant systems. Convectors are typically smaller, and baseboards are typically much smaller. Not surprisingly, it takes a greater length of baseboard to deliver the same amount of heat as one 3-foot long radiator.

Frying Pan Analogy   If you think of cast-iron radiators and copper-tube convectors, we can make an analogy to frying pans. Those who have cooked with a cast-iron frying pan know

F I G U R E 4.4   Finned Tube Baseboard

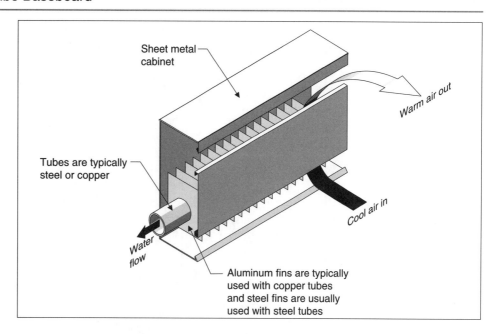

that it takes quite a while to heat it up. However, once it's heated, it retains its heat for a long time. A copper or aluminum frying pan heats up very quickly but also cools off very quickly.

This analogy works for heating systems as well. Cast-iron radiators take a long time to heat up, but once they get hot, they stay hot. Copper-tube baseboards can heat up much more quickly, but also cool down much more quickly when the boiler shuts off.

Heats Up Slowly, Cools Down Slowly

Many homes are uncomfortable because they have a combination of radiators and baseboards. If the thermostat is located in a part of the house where there are radiators, the thermostat will respond to the heat given off by the radiators. When the thermostat calls for heat, it will take a while for the thermostat to see the heat from the radiators. However, once the room gets warm, it will tend to stay warm and the thermostat will stay satisfied for a long time. This leads to longer on cycles and longer off cycles for the boiler.

Mixing Systems Yields Uncomfortable Heating

If the same house has baseboards in another part, remote from the thermostat, when the thermostat calls for heat, the baseboards respond quickly and deliver heat to the room fast. This means the room gets comfortable right away. However, since the thermostat is waiting for the cast-iron radiators to warm up, the boiler keeps running. The room with baseboards may actually overheat (Figure 4.5).

Overheat

When the cast-iron radiators finally get hot and the thermostat is satisfied, the boiler shuts off. The room with the baseboards cools down very quickly and becomes uncomfortable. The room with the radiator is still warm and cozy. The thermostat doesn't see the need for more heat.

Underheat

As you can see, houses with these combinations can be difficult to heat comfortably.

Think about the same house but put the thermostat in the room with the baseboards. What do you think will happen?

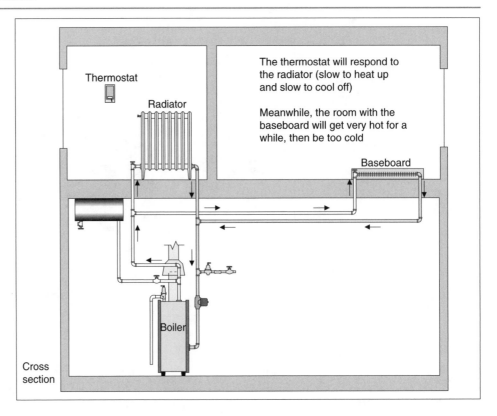

4.2   LOCATION OF RADIATORS

Under Windows

In much the same way as our heating philosophy worked with forced air, it's best to put the radiators on outside walls below windows. Since this tends to be the coolest part of the room, it makes sense to put most of the heat here. That gives us the most even heating across the room.

Convective Loop

We don't have a return air system with hot water, but we do have a convective loop set up in the room. The heavy, cool air is drawn across the floor toward the radiator. The light, warm air is directed up across the cool windows and out into the room. This system works well and provides even heat.

Why Are Radiators Sometimes on Ceilings

Older heating systems were usually convection (gravity) systems. They did not have pumps to push the water through the system. Where the boiler was located in a basement, people often finished portions of the basement. They wanted to heat these rooms. Since the heat moved only by convection, putting a radiator in the floor in a basement room adjacent to the boiler room was not very effective.

Or High on the Walls?

This radiator would stay filled with cold water, which was heavy. There would be no incentive for convective flow.

Heat from Boiler Moves up

People had to put the radiators high up in these rooms so that the water in the radiators would be above the boiler (Figure 4.6). This allowed for convective flow, with the cold water falling back down toward the boiler and the lighter, hot water moving to the radiator.

Putting the heat into a room near the ceiling level was a compromise on ideal design, but at least it got some heat into the room.

Auxiliary Heat, the Practicality of It All

One of the downsides of hot water heating is that it's very expensive to upgrade the system. Adding a radiator typically costs several hundred dollars. Where a cool

FIGURE 4.6 Radiators on Ceilings or High Walls

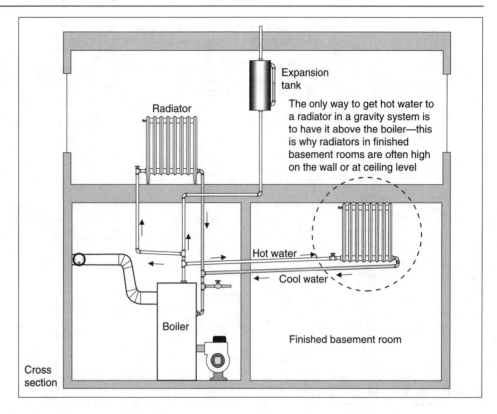

area is identified in a home with hot water heating, it's often more practical to add an electric baseboard heater.

4.3 BALANCING VALVES

We touched on **balancing valves** earlier. In most two-pipe systems, most of the radiators have balancing valves. Small radiators in the vestibules and washrooms, for example, may not have balancing valves. The important thing for home inspectors to know about balancing valves is that they should never touch them!

They'll Leak!

These valves are not operated on a regular basis. As soon as you turn them, they usually leak. Unless you're prepared to do some emergency repair work, we recommend that you leave them alone.

Look but Don't Touch

We do recommend that you have a close look at the valves and at the piping and flooring below. It's common to find considerable damage here. The leaks at these balancing valves can be particularly troublesome because they're often minor and can go unnoticed for some time. They can do a fair bit of damage to the woodwork and other components below while this is going on (Figure 4.7).

4.4 BLEED VALVES

Air bleed valves should be located near the top of every radiator to let trapped air out so the water can circulate properly.

F I G U R E 4.7   Radiator Valve Leaks

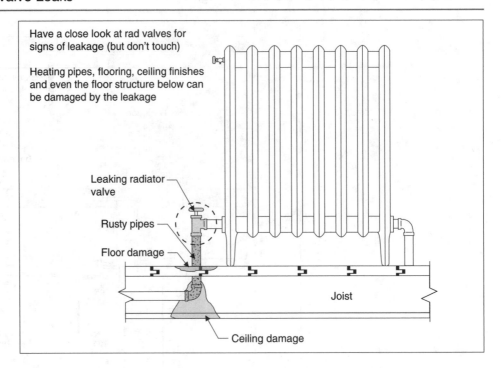

Have a close look at rad valves for signs of leakage (but don't touch)

Heating pipes, flooring, ceiling finishes and even the floor structure below can be damaged by the leakage

Leaking radiator valve

Rusty pipes

Floor damage

Joist

Ceiling damage

F I G U R E 4.8   Don't Operate Air Bleed Valves

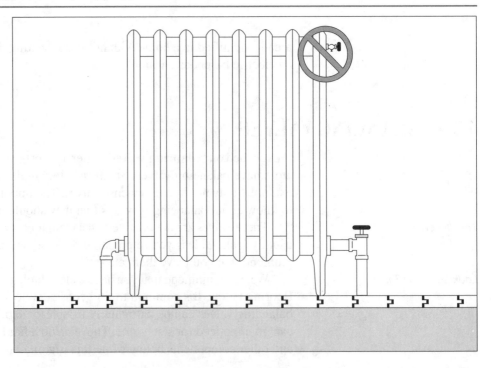

Manual—Hand Operated   These valves are usually manual. The valve stem doesn't have to be removed, just loosened. As soon as air starts to rush out, the valve is usually left open until water comes out. As soon as water is delivered, the valve is closed.

Don't Open   Again, we urge you not to operate these valves, although it's pretty tempting sometimes (Figure 4.8).

4.5   ZONED SYSTEMS

Several Small Houses

Mixing Radiators and Baseboards

We talked earlier about how hot water heating systems can be zoned. These systems have multiple thermostats and can use multiple circulating pumps or zone valves to deliver heat to the different parts of the house at different times.

The radiators, convectors, and baseboards perform the same way on a zoned system, and you can simply think of these as several small house systems.

A zoned system is one application where you might get away with radiators on one thermostat and convectors or baseboards on a different thermostat. In fact, this can be a solution to a problem house with radiators in an old part and baseboards in a new part. Setting up a zoned system can allow both parts of the house to be kept comfortable.

4.6   CONDITIONS

Radiators, convectors, and baseboards should be checked for these problems:

1. Leaks
2. Rust
3. Too small
4. Missing
5. Poor location
6. Mixed types
7. Balancing valve problems
8. Bleed valve problems
9. Damaged baseboard fins
10. Obstructed air flow

4.6.1   Leaks

CAUSES

IMPLICATIONS

STRATEGY

Radiators may leak because of rust, mechanical damage, or poor connections. As we mentioned, they are most likely to leak at their balancing valves.

The implications of a leak are water damage to the home and, possibly, a no-heat condition if considerable water is lost.

Check closely at the balancing valves and bleed valves for evidence of leakage.

4.6.2   Rust

CAUSES AND IMPLICATIONS

STRATEGY

We've talked about the causes and implications of rust.

Look for rust at radiators, convectors, and baseboards. Again, it's most common around the balancing valve.

4.6.3   Too Small

CAUSES

This is an installation issue. It can be the result of a room extension, or additional glass (skylights, solariums, sliding doors, etc) added to a room.

IMPLICATIONS

The room will be uncomfortable.

STRATEGY

You aren't going to do a design analysis of the adequacy of the radiators for each room. The standards don't require this. What you can use is a little bit of common sense. Pay some attention to the average size and number of the radiators and the average room size as you go through the house. If you see one that is obviously out of step, you should at least raise the question about the comfort of this room.

As we mentioned earlier, it may be more cost effective to add electric baseboard heat than to extend a hot water heating system. It's expensive to add more radiators, convectors, or baseboards.

4.6.4   Missing

This is an easy one to overlook.

CAUSES

Missing radiators are usually radiators that have been removed during renovations. Since radiators are bulky, they can be in the way. Sometimes they are removed and there are no replacements.

We find it common to have a kitchen radiator removed and not replaced. Kitchens tend to be warm rooms because of the heat given off by the refrigerator and cooking appliances.

IMPLICATION

The implication is inadequate heat.

STRATEGY

Look for a heating source in each room. In some cases, you can find capped pipes, filled pipe holes in floors, or stained flooring where the radiator used to be. Point out to your client the absence of the heat source, and prepare them for the possibility that the heating will be inadequate.

4.6.5   Poor Location

CAUSES

We talked about why we sometimes find radiators high on walls or on ceilings in basements. In other cases, radiators are poorly located because of poor initial installation or room rearrangement during renovations.

Radiators can be obstructed by furniture, drapes, or radiator covers. All these reduce the heating efficiency and may make the room uncomfortable.

IMPLICATIONS

If the radiators are not located on exterior walls below windows, the room may be uncomfortable. On rooms with many windows, it is sometimes more desirable to use a long, low-profile convector, baseboard, or wall-mounted radiator than one or two large radiators. Because there is a great length of the room that's likely to be cool, the heating source should be extended along the same length.

STRATEGY

Where radiators are located on interior walls or are not below windows, point out the possible comfort effects. Again, talk about how auxiliary heat can be added relatively inexpensively, if necessary.

4.6.6   Mixed Types

CAUSES

Combining radiators with convectors or baseboards is generally considered poor practice but is often done when additions are put on.

IMPLICATIONS

We've talked about the comfort implications of mixing various types. Some rooms may get too hot and then get too cold, while other rooms are consistently comfortable.

STRATEGY

Note the type of heating distribution and let your client know of the possible comfort implications.

4.6.7   Balancing Valve Problems

CAUSES

Problems with these valves are caused by lack of regular operation. The valves become frozen and the packing leaks when people try to operate them. In some cases, handles can be broken or missing, and the valve body can be corroded by rust from around the packing.

IMPLICATIONS

The implications include water damage. If the valves can't be adjusted, the implication also is poor comfort. If the leakage has damaged the piping or valve body, expensive repairs may be necessary.

STRATEGY

We've already told you to look closely at these valves. We're emphasizing it here because most of us forget, from time to time.

4.6.8   Bleed Valve Problems

CAUSES

These valves are operated more frequently than the balancing valves and, as a result, are less problematic. However, the valves can be painted closed. The valve handles and valve stems are fragile and are intended to be operated by hand. Wrenches and pliers can damage the bleed valves.

IMPLICATIONS

Flooding is one implication of a bleed valve problem. Poor comfort is another, if you can't bleed the air out of the radiator.

STRATEGY

Look for evidence of leakage. This is most often a streak running down the radiator from the bleed valves. Look also for active leakage and mechanical damage to the valve or handle itself.

4.6.9   Damaged Baseboard Fins

CAUSE

Mechanical damage is common to fins on baseboard heaters. This is particularly true of aluminum fins but can also be an issue on copper or steel fins.

Damage normally occurs after the cover has been knocked off.

IMPLICATIONS

Reduced heating capacity and efficiency are the implications.

STRATEGY

Make sure covers are in place on baseboards. Where they are loose or missing, recommend they be resecured and check the fins for damage.

If you can look into baseboards without removing the covers, check the condition of the fins. Fins flattened or bent can be straightened in most cases. There are "fin combs" available to do this.

4.6.10   Obstructed Air Flow

CAUSE

Convectors and radiators may be obstructed with furniture, drapes, or decorative covers. In many cases, the performance is still adequate. Baseboards may have their bottom inlets obstructed by carpeting, for example. This can dramatically affect their heating capacity.

| IMPLICATIONS | Obstructed baseboards may result in cold rooms. |
| STRATEGY | Look at the bottom of baseboard heaters. Are the intakes open or obstructed? If obstructed, advise your client that simply cutting the carpet back may make the room much more comfortable. |

CHAPTER REVIEW QUESTIONS

Answer the following questions on a separate sheet of paper, then check your results against the answers provided in Appendix E. If you have trouble with a question, refer back to the chapter to review the relevant material.

1. List three styles of heat delivery that are used with boilers.

2. Mixing convectors and radiators in a single hydronic system will often result in uncomfortable heating.

    True   False

3. Where should a radiator be placed in a room?

    a. On an interior wall

    b. On an exterior wall

    c. On an exterior wall below a window

    d. On the ceiling

    e. It doesn't matter; the radiator radiates heat to the room from any location

4. What is the purpose of the bleed valve near the top of the radiator?

5. Why do balancing valves tend to leak when operated?

KEY TERMS

| radiator | baseboard | balancing valve |
| convector | | |

CHAPTER

RADIANT HEATING AND TANKLESS COILS

LEARNING OBJECTIVES

At the end of this chapter you should be able to:

■ list the four problems found with radiant heating

■ list the four problems found with tankless coils

5.1   RADIANT HEATING

Some hot water heating systems don't have any radiators, convectors, or base-boards. Pipes are buried in the ceilings, walls, and/or floors (Figure 5.1). Piping embedded in the plaster ceilings is considered one of the most desirable applications.

High-Quality Systems

These systems are often considered desirable because they are capable of delivering very even heat. They are generally expensive to install but can provide excellent, even heating.

Materials

The piping can be wrought iron, steel, copper, or plastic, including polybutylene and polyethylene. The steel and wrought iron are typically only used for floors. They are too heavy for walls and ceilings.

Pipe Size

The piping can be anywhere from $1/4$ inch to 1 inch in diameter. The pipes are laid in grids or coils. The spacing between adjacent pipes should never be more than 12 inches and can be as close as 4 to 6 inches.

Temperature Is an Issue

In a room with 8-foot ceilings, the maximum temperature desired is about 110°F. If the ceilings get warmer than that, they can be uncomfortably warm. When piping is buried in floors, you don't want the temperature above about 85°F.

Water Can't Be Too Hot

This creates a challenge for boiler systems. With radiators, convectors, and baseboards, we don't usually worry about the water at the boiler being too hot. However, with radiant systems, we normally run the boiler water around 120°F to 130°F. This is relatively cool.

Water Blender

These low temperatures are often achieved by using a water blender (Figure 5.2). This mixes some cold water with the hot water coming off the boiler to achieve a desired temperature. These are also called mixing valves or tempering valves.

F I G U R E 5.1   Hot Water Radiant Heat

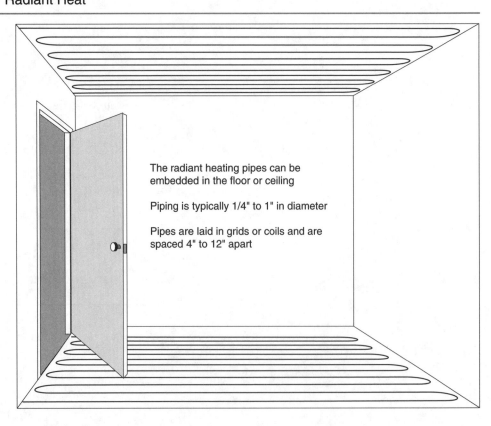

The radiant heating pipes can be embedded in the floor or ceiling

Piping is typically 1/4" to 1" in diameter

Pipes are laid in grids or coils and are spaced 4" to 12" apart

FIGURE 5.2   Water Blender on Radiant System

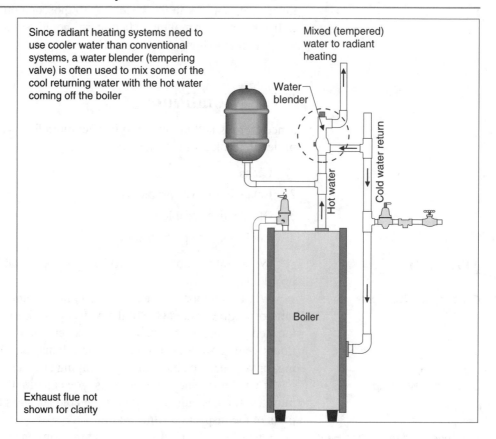

Since radiant heating systems need to use cooler water than conventional systems, a water blender (tempering valve) is often used to mix some of the cool returning water with the hot water coming off the boiler

Mixed (tempered) water to radiant heating

Water blender

Hot water

Cold water return

Boiler

Exhaust flue not shown for clarity

Outdoor Thermostat

Some houses with radiant hot water heating do not use conventional thermostats. An outdoor temperature sensor reads the exterior temperature and adjusts the water blender to deliver the right temperature water through the radiant system. Water continuously circulates through the radiant system and the water temperature is adjusted based on the outdoor temperature.

Air Bleeds and Zone Controls

Radiant heating systems need to have the air bled out. Bleed valves are usually located in concealed panels throughout the house. They are usually at the high points, where the air bubbles collect.

Balancing Valves

There are often control valves that can be adjusted manually to balance the heating system. They can also be isolating valves, in some cases. Again, these can be located throughout the house and well concealed or may be adjacent to the boiler.

It's great to have a schematic drawing of the layout of the radiant heating system. This can help to achieve good balance and to find isolating valves to do localized repairs.

One has to be careful drilling into ceilings or floors with radiant systems. You don't want to puncture a pipe.

Hot Spots and Cold Spots

Hot spots on floors can be a problem, especially if the pipes are far apart. If your foot is right on a pipe, it can be quite warm. The area between two pipes can be considerably cooler.

Leaks

Leaks in these systems can cause a lot of damage. Leaks in concrete floor slabs can be tough to find. Considerable erosion of the soil under a slab may take place while the leak is unnoticed.

Service people look for leaks in radiant systems buried in floors by shutting off the connection to the plumbing system so that no water can be added. The pressure gauge at the boiler is watched with the boiler at rest. If the pressure drops over time, this suggests a leak in the system. A stethoscope on the piping is sometimes used to listen for water moving, when there should be none. This is not something that we recommend home inspectors do.

5.1.1 Conditions

Since there is nothing much to inspect on radiant systems, we won't go into a lot of detail. Look for the following:

1. Leaks
2. Balancing valves problems
3. Bleed valves problems
4. Cool rooms or parts of rooms

STRATEGY

Checking for Cool Spots

We've talked about how to look for leaks and balancing and bleed valve problems.

While cool rooms are easy to detect in the winter, this can be a challenge in the mild or warm weather. One of the ways to check a radiant system is to feel the surface temperature. First you have to discover where the **radiant piping** is. Is it in the floors, ceiling, walls, or a combination? You may be told, you may find a layout drawing, or you may be able to trace the piping and the valves.

Let System Warm up

If you know where the piping is, you can turn the thermostat(s) up and wait 45 minutes. It takes quite a while for the cold surfaces to warm up. You can do other parts of the inspection while waiting.

Use Your Hand To Feel the Heat

Once the system is up to temperature, you can feel the ceiling (for example) surfaces to see if they are warm to the touch. Since rooms may be zoned, some inspectors test the four corners of each room. An inactive area can be felt.

Clean Hands

We recommend that your hands be clean while doing this. Use the back of your hand to sense the heat. Because pipes can be several inches apart, you may have to move your hand across the surface to find the heat.

The danger of doing this in warm weather is that you'll make the house uncomfortably warm. It will take some time to cool. Ask permission before doing this test in the summer.

5.2 TANKLESS COILS

Tankless coils are properly a domestic water heater. We touch on them briefly so you will know what you're looking at when you see them.

Normally, we have a separate water heater with its own burner and storage tank. Sometimes the boiler is also used to heat the domestic hot water. When we use the heating boiler to provide hot water, we have neither a storage tank nor a separate burner.

Tankless Coil or Indirect Water Heater

The tankless coil is a heat exchanger that brings cold water from the supply plumbing piping into the boiler (Figure 5.3). The water is heated by the boiler and is sent out through the hot water supply plumbing distribution system. We are running the supply plumbing through the boiler to heat up the water for washing dishes, washing clothes, having showers, taking baths, etc. This is called an indirect water heater.

FIGURE 5.3 Tankless Coil

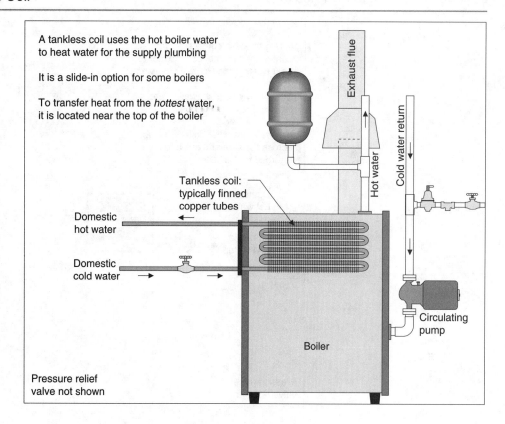

A tankless coil uses the hot boiler water to heat water for the supply plumbing

It is a slide-in option for some boilers

To transfer heat from the *hottest* water, it is located near the top of the boiler

Tankless coil: typically finned copper tubes

Domestic hot water

Domestic cold water

Exhaust flue

Hot water

Cold water return

Circulating pump

Boiler

Pressure relief valve not shown

| Option on Some Boilers | These coils are typically a slide-in option on boilers. Not all boilers can accept a tankless coil. |

Option on Some Boilers

These coils are typically a slide-in option on boilers. Not all boilers can accept a tankless coil.

Side-Arm Heaters

The **side-arm heater** is a variation on the tankless coil. It's a coil mounted outside the boiler (Figure 5.4). The boiler water comes out of the boiler and heats the domestic water. The boiler water then returns to the boiler.

The side-arm heater works the same as the tankless coil. The difference is the heat exchanger is external to the boiler. These are less common on modern systems.

Storage Tank Optional

Tankless coils can feed water directly to the hot water supply piping or can go to a storage tank.

Mixing Valve

Some tankless coils require a mixing valve to cool the water so that it will not scald people. Some cold water is mixed with the hot water coming out of the coil before it's distributed to the house. Mixing valves can be thermostatically controlled to deliver water at a desired temperature (eg, 130°F).

Advantages

There are several advantages to tankless coils:

1. The coils last a long time since they don't see flame temperatures or products of combustion. They see water on both sides.

2. The coils are less susceptible to scaling than if they saw higher temperatures from combustion products on the other side.

3. There is no need for a storage tank.

4. There is no need for a separate burner with controls, venting, and combustion air requirements.

Disadvantages

There are also disadvantages:

1. The boiler may wear out sooner because it has to stay hot all summer. (Boilers are more expensive than water heaters.)

F I G U R E 5.4   Side-Arm Heater

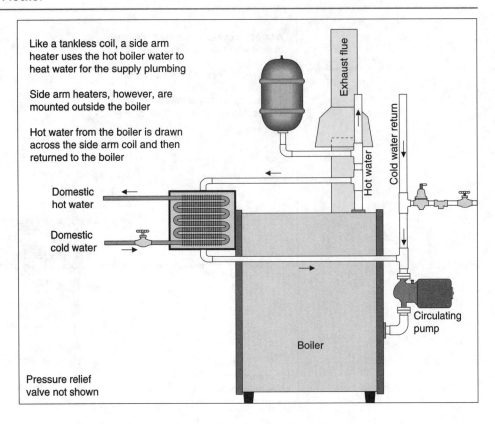

Like a tankless coil, a side arm heater uses the hot boiler water to heat water for the supply plumbing

Side arm heaters, however, are mounted outside the boiler

Hot water from the boiler is drawn across the side arm coil and then returned to the boiler

Domestic hot water

Domestic cold water

Exhaust flue

Hot water

Cold water return

Circulating pump

Boiler

Pressure relief valve not shown

2. The domestic water may be too hot if the mixing valve is missing or defective.

3. The domestic water can be too cold if the boiler water is too cold.

4. The system may be inefficient if the boiler is not as well insulated as a water heater.

5. The boiler room may overheat during the summer.

6. The domestic water may be contaminated by boiler water if the coil leaks.

7. The boiler system may be overpressurized if the coil leaks.

8. The boiler may not be large enough to meet peak space heating and water heating demands at the same time.

5.2.1 Conditions

We'll look very briefly at the problems you might come across in tankless coils.

1. Leaks

2. Rust

3. Clogged

4. No mixing valve or mixing valve set incorrectly

Leaks

CAUSES

Leaks are typically caused by corrosion or metal fatigue.

IMPLICATIONS

A leaking tankless coil can lead to a cross connection between the potable (drinking) water of the plumbing system and the contaminated boiler water. A leaking tankless coil can also overpressurize the heating system, causing the pressure-relief valve to discharge. If the pressure-relief valve doesn't discharge properly, we can generate a superheated water situation, which is a safety issue.

STRATEGY

Look for leaks around the coil plate where it fits into the boiler and at the piping connections.

Rust

CAUSE

Rust is caused by oxygen and water and/or chemicals in the water.

IMPLICATIONS

The implications of rust are leakage.

STRATEGY

Look for rust streaking at the coil faceplate or the piping connections.

Clogged

CAUSES

Clogged coils are the result of mineral build-up inside the coils.

IMPLICATIONS

Clogged coils result in poor hot water pressure throughout the home.

STRATEGY

You won't be able to see clogged coils directly. Your test of the plumbing system will help to reveal clogged coils.

Mixing Valve Missing, Set Wrong, or Defective

This is an installation or adjustment problem.

CAUSES

IMPLICATIONS

Implications include—

1. Scalding people if there is no mixing valve, or if the valve is set too high or is defective

2. Water not hot enough if the valve is set too low or is defective

STRATEGY

You can get a sense of the temperature when you run the domestic hot water as part of your plumbing inspection. Some inspectors measure the water temperatures.

You can see if there is no mixing valve.

CHAPTER REVIEW QUESTIONS

Answer the following questions on a separate sheet of paper, then check your results against the answers provided in Appendix E. If you have trouble with a question, refer back to the chapter to review the relevant material.

1. What is the maximum ceiling temperature you would want to have in an 8-foot room with radiant pipe heating?

   a. 70°F

   b. 90°F

   c. 110°F

   d. 130°F

   e. 150°F

2. Describe a procedure that can be used to check for leaking radiant floor piping.

3. Do radiant piping systems need bleed valves, since there are no radiators?
Yes   No

4. Why is a tankless coil water heater called an indirect water heater?

5. Explain how a side-arm heater is different from the tankless coil.

6. Boilers with tankless coil domestic water heaters are inefficient because

   a. the coil is susceptible to scaling.

   b. the boiler water is too cold to provide adequate hot domestic water.

   c. the boiler needs to stay hot all summer.

   d. contamination can occur between the boiler water and the domestic water.

   e. it is difficult to find a boiler large enough to meet peak space heating and domestic water heating demands.

7. Why would you have a mixing valve on a tankless coil heater?

KEY TERMS

radiant piping   tankless coil   side-arm heater

CHAPTER 6

MID- AND HIGH-EFFICIENCY BOILERS AND COMBINATION SYSTEMS

LEARNING OBJECTIVES

At the end of this chapter you should be able to:

■ list the problems found with high-efficiency boilers

■ list the problems found with combination systems

6.1   MID-EFFICIENCY BOILERS

Boilers have undergone similar changes to furnaces during the past 20 years. The changes have been slower in some cases, and there are fewer residential boilers than furnaces to choose from, so the efficiency choices are more limited.

Putting a Sock in the Chimney

"Putting a sock in the chimney" was the first step for furnaces. It was also the first step for boilers. For many manufacturers, it is the only step they have taken. Automatic vent dampers and electronic ignition are common improvements.

Spillage Switch

One feature found on many mid-efficiency boilers is a heat-sensing (spillage) switch at the draft hood. If the vent damper fails to open, or the chimney is obstructed, for example, exhaust gases may spill out through the draft hood. The spillage switch senses the high temperature and shuts off the burner (Figure 6.1).

Induced Draft

Some boilers use an induced-draft fan, just like the mid-efficiency furnaces. Other mid-efficiency boilers use a forced-draft fan and some have condensate drains to allow for condensation, although they are not true condensing boilers.

Safety Controls

The induced-draft and forced-draft boilers have the same safety controls (purge and proving-air movement through the venting system, for example) as induced-draft furnaces.

Intermittent Pilot

Boilers often have spark ignition systems for the pilot flame, so the pilot doesn't have to burn constantly. This efficiency improvement is the same one we discussed on mid-efficiency furnaces.

Bypass Loop

Some boilers have an integral bypass or mixing valve. This directs some of the hot water from the boiler into the return piping just as it enters the boiler, minimizing thermal shock and condensation on the combustion side of the heat exchanger (Figure 6.2).

These bypass loops can also be added by the system installer.

Venting Materials and Clearances

Combustion products are hot. Galvanized or stainless steel vents with 6-inch clearances from combustibles are typical for gas and 9-inch to 18-inch clearances

FIGURE 6.1   Spillage Switch

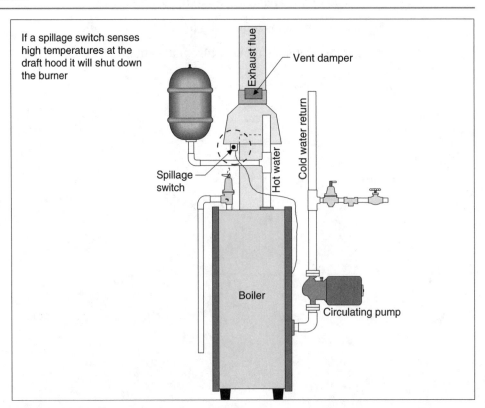

FIGURE 6.2 Bypass Loop

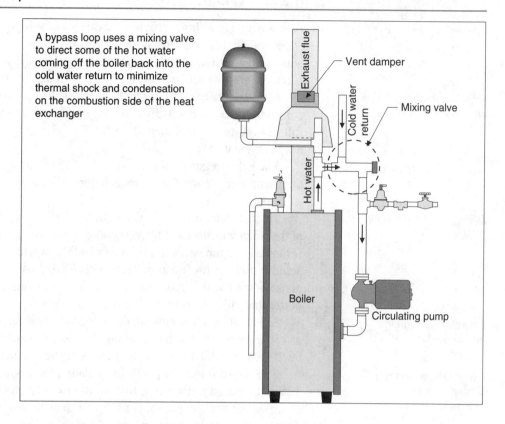

A bypass loop uses a mixing valve to direct some of the hot water coming off the boiler back into the cold water return to minimize thermal shock and condensation on the combustion side of the heat exchanger

Exhaust flue

Vent damper

Cold water return

Mixing valve

Hot water

Boiler

Circulating pump

for oil. The high-temperature plastic vents (Plexvent, Sel-Vent, Ultravent) may be used. Their performance is suspect in some jurisdictions. There are bans and recalls on these products.

6.2   HIGH-EFFICIENCY BOILERS

High-efficiency boilers are not as common as high-efficiency furnaces. High-efficiency boilers can be twice the cost of regular boilers, while high-efficiency furnaces cost only 30 to 40 percent more than lower-efficiency systems. There are fewer manufacturers of high-efficiency boiler equipment. Let's look at some of the advantages and disadvantages of high-efficiency hot water heating.

6.2.1   Advantages

No Chimney Needed

High-efficiency equipment needs no traditional chimneys. The combustion products are vented out through the house wall, typically through a plastic or metal vent.

Direct Vent

High-efficiency boilers are typically direct vent systems. Not only do the exhaust gases go straight through the wall, but combustion air is piped in from outside, and the combustion chamber is sealed from the house air.

Low Operating Costs

The operating costs of high-efficiency boilers are considerably lower than those of conventional boilers. Seasonal efficiencies in the range of 85 percent to 95 percent are possible. The seasonal efficiency of conventional boilers may be 55 percent to 65 percent.

6.2.2   Disadvantages

Costly
Condensation

A disadvantage of high-efficiency boilers is the high installation cost.

Another disadvantage is the corrosion issue that comes up anytime we deal with condensation. In a high-efficiency boiler, just like a high-efficiency furnace, corrosion may occur because it produces an acidic condensate.

High Maintenance Costs
and Poor Reliability

Maintenance costs for high-efficiency boilers are typically much higher than with conventional equipment. Just like high-efficiency furnaces, they are complex and full of high-tech components. So far, the reliability of high-efficiency boilers has not been great.

The exhaust gas path through the heat exchanger is longer and more restricted than with conventional heat exchangers. We expect problems with clogged heat exchangers.

Mismatch with Distribution
System

Another common difficulty with high-efficiency boilers is the incompatibility of the boiler with the existing distribution system. You'll remember that high-efficiency furnaces used the latent heat of vaporization to grab heat from the exhaust gases, to achieve their high-efficiency ratings. The combustion products of natural gas condense when the flue gas temperature drops to roughly 125°F. If the flue gases are hotter than this, the boiler will not condense, and the efficiency is diminished.

Radiators Designed
for Hot Water

Many radiator systems are designed to be supplied with water leaving the boiler at 150°F to 200°F. The temperature drop as the water goes through the system may be 20°F to 30°F. This is a typical temperature rise across a boiler, as well.

Return Water Too Hot To
Cause Exhaust
Gases To Condense

The return water temperature in many piping systems may well be higher than 125°F. Obviously, it's tough to cool the exhaust gases below the dew point if the water side of the heat exchanger is hotter than the dew point. Sometimes we get condensation at startup, but none when the system heats up to steady state.

Small-Volume Boilers

Another difficulty encountered with high-efficiency boilers is the small heat exchanger volumes. Traditional boilers held several gallons of water. In most high-efficiency boilers, the volume is much smaller. This can cause problems. The rate of water flow through the boiler is critical on high-efficiency systems. The boiler may overheat if the water flow rate is not adequate.

Different Pumps

Typically, the water flow requirements of high-efficiency boilers are considerably higher than those of conventional boilers. As the water must move through the pipes faster, increasing the friction losses in the piping, the pump capacity of the new boiler may have to be considerably larger than the old pump. This needs to be sized for the existing distribution system.

Short Cycling

It's not easy for the boiler manufacturer to determine what pump is needed for all systems. If the boiler overheats because the water flow is too slow, the boiler will short cycle. This means that the burner will go off and on several times before the thermostat is satisfied. This shortens the life of the heat exchanger and wears out the mechanical components in the system faster.

Similarities to High-Efficiency
Furnace

High-efficiency boilers use many of the same components that high-efficiency furnaces do. There is often a second heat exchanger. In addition, there is some form of intermittent ignition and a low-temperature venting system. Because the ignition systems are the same, the safety controls are also similar.

Forced-Draft Rather than
Induced Draft

Boilers tend to differ from furnaces in that there are some forced-draft, high-efficiency boilers. So far, forced-draft technology has not been widely used in high-efficiency furnaces.

Cupro-Nickel Heat Exchangers

Heat exchanger material is also different in some instances. Stainless steel is a common heat exchanger material for both boilers and furnaces, but some boilers are also made from copper-nickel alloys (eg, cupro-nickel). These alloys are more corrosion resistant than stainless steel and have good thermal-conducting properties.

Pulse Systems

Pulse combustion is used on the Hydrotherm HydroPulse or MultiPulse boiler, a high-efficiency hot water system. There is no burner, no pilot, no vent connector, and no chimney. Figure 6.3 summarizes how the system works.

Direct Vent

This is a direct vent system that uses PVC pipe (aluminum dryer vent or galvanized steel is also used in some areas) to bring combustion air from the outside into the sealed combustion chamber. Exhaust is sidewall vented through CPVC pipe, typically $1^1/_2$- to 3-inch diameter. The pipe size depends on the boiler capacity and the length of the vent. Both intake and vent pipes should slope down toward the boiler at $1/_4$ inch per foot of length on the horizontal runs. Piping should be supported every 5 feet (in Canada, every 3 feet).

Condensing

The HydroPulse is a condensing boiler and uses condensate drain piping.

Noise

HydroPulse boilers, like Pulse furnaces, can be noisy. Vibration damping connectors on the distribution piping are often used to minimize the noise and vibration throughout the house.

Mufflers can be used on the exterior of the house to reduce the outdoor noise.

6.2.3   Efficiency

Condensing boilers have efficiency ratings of over 90 percent. Noncondensing or partially condensing boilers have efficiencies in the 80 to 88 percent range.

6.2.4   Conditions

High-efficiency boiler problems are:

1. Cabinet problems
2. Fuel supply and burner problems
3. Combustion air and venting problems
4. Ignition problems
5. Heat exchanger problems
6. Safety and operating control problems
7. Induced-draft and forced-draft fan problems
8. Condensate handling problems
9. Distribution system problems (expansion tanks, pumps, piping, radiators, convectors, and baseboards)
10. Inadequate water flow rate through the boiler. (This problem is unique to high-efficiency boilers. You won't be able to recognize it during a home inspection.)
11. Noise (Noisy operation is easy to detect. This is most common on pulse systems. This can be an issue inside and outside of the home.)

6.3   COMBINATION SYSTEMS

Some of the high-efficiency boilers are also designed to heat the domestic hot water. We talked earlier about the tankless coils, which are **combination systems.** Modern systems typically use a coil in a water storage tank rather than a coil in the boiler.

FIGURE 6.3   Pulse Combination—How It Works

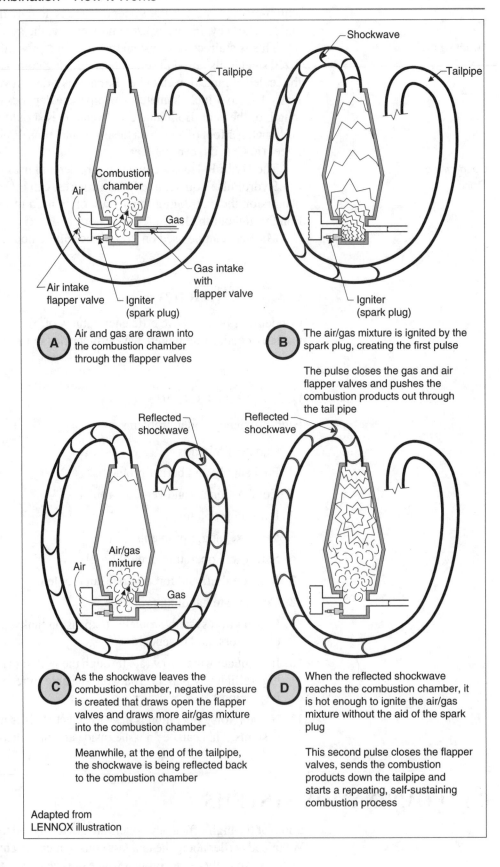

Hot water from the boiler is pumped through a coil in the water storage tank, heating the domestic water. There are various arrangements, but the goal is to use a high-efficiency heating system to provide both space heating and water heating.

6.3.1   Conditions

It is too early to know what the long-term performance of the modern combination systems is going to be. If we look at tankless coils, we may get some hints. Problems may include the following:

1. Potable water mixes with contaminated boiler water if coils leak.
2. Boiler systems may be pressurized by plumbing system water if coils leak.
3. If there is no heat, there is no hot water.
4. The boiler life expectancy may be reduced if the boiler has to fire year round instead of during the winter only. Conventional water heaters are not expensive to replace; boilers are.
5. Boilers staying hot in a standby mode to provide domestic hot water may be inefficient, especially if the boiler is not as well insulated as a conventional water heater.
6. The living space around the hot boiler may be overheated in the summer.
7. The boiler may not have adequate capacity to provide both space heating and domestic water heating during cold weather combined with high domestic water demands.

We suspect there are other issues lurking out there. In a sense, our job is simple. Determine whether the system is doing its job. If the house is warm and there is hot water, you've met a minimum standard. Going beyond this may be very risky, unless you have special training or at least in-depth knowledge of the system you're inspecting.

CHAPTER REVIEW QUESTIONS

Answer the following questions on a separate sheet of paper, then check your results against the answers provided in Appendix E. If you have trouble with a question, refer back to the chapter to review the relevant material.

1. What two improvements can be made to a boiler to make it a mid-efficiency boiler?
2. What are three possible advantages of high-efficiency hot water boilers?
3. What are some of the design and operating challenges of high-efficiency boilers?
4. List six common problems with high-efficiency boilers. Include one problem unique to high-efficiency boilers.
5. What is the difference between a combination system and a tankless coil system?

KEY TERMS   high-efficiency   combination system

CHAPTER

LIFE EXPECTANCY, CAPACITY, AND SEQUENCE OF OPERATIONS

LEARNING OBJECTIVES

At the end of this chapter you should be able to:

■ list and briefly describe the steps in the sequence of operation of a hot water boiler

■ understand how long different boilers last

■ understand how to use a general rule to determine the adequacy of the boiler capacity

7.1   LIFE EXPECTANCY

Cast Iron

Old cast-iron boilers commonly have a **life expectancy** of 35 to 50 years. We have seen 80-year-old boilers still in service. These systems were originally fired with coal. They were often converted to oil, and later changed to gas.

Converted from Steam to Hot Water

Some old boilers were designed as steam systems and have been converted to hot water. This may not be apparent during a home inspection and apart from interest does not matter to the inspector or homeowner.

Old Steel Boilers

Some older steel boilers typically lasted 20 to 35 years, although most of those are near the end of their life now.

Newer Steel Boilers

The lighter steel and the copper-tube boilers have life expectancies of 15 to 25 years. Some fail as early as 10 years into their life, and there are always those that do better.

Condensation High-Tech Boilers

Condensation causing rust is the big enemy of both the steel and copper-tube boilers. No one knows for sure how well the newer high-efficiency boilers are going to perform over the long term. Heat exchangers are typically copper, stainless steel, or cupro-nickel alloys. Some difficulties have been experienced with the copper heat exchangers on some systems. These are being replaced with stainless steel as they fail.

7.2   CAPACITY

Most residential boilers are oversized. It's unusual to find a boiler that is too small for a house. This can happen, for example, when an addition is put on a house.

No Heat Loss Calculations

Home inspectors do not evaluate the heating system adequacy based on detailed heat loss calculations; it takes a few hours and is well beyond our scope. We will look at making a rough approximation. Where you suspect a heating system is undersized, you will probably recommend further investigation rather than additional heat or replacement of the heating system.

Boiler Oversized Most Days

Most boilers are designed to keep the house warm on the coldest day of the year. Consequently, the boiler is oversized every other day of the year.

The design temperature for a heating system is determined by your location. Across the northern half of North America, design temperatures can range from 25°F to 65°F. In southern climates, the design temperature will be higher.

The Perfectly Sized Boiler

A perfectly sized boiler would run continuously on the coldest day, adding heat to the home at exactly the same rate that it is being lost from the home. If the boiler is just slightly undersized, the house will get cold, and heating contractors will get complaints.

Heating contractors don't like complaints. Therefore, most heating systems are oversized. A slightly larger boiler rarely costs significantly more money, and the risk of having a boiler that is slightly undersized simply isn't worth it.

The size of the boiler depends on several factors, including:

Several Variables

- the climate (as we have discussed)
- the size of the house
- how quickly the house loses heat (insulation and weather-tightness)
- the output capacity of the heating system (steady-state efficiency)
- lifestyle of the homeowners and amount of other heat generated in the home

A General Rule

In the middle part of North America, we find that modern homes need roughly 20 to 30 BTUs per square foot. Older homes (typically poorly insulated and not very weather-tight) need 30 to 60 BTU per square foot.

Careful

Like all good guidelines, these should be used with extreme caution. Remember that we are talking about the output capacity of the boiler rather than the input capacity or firing rate.

Check for Auxiliary Heat

Where a guideline indicates that a heating system may be undersized, look for auxiliary sources of heat. There may be electric baseboard heaters, for instance. Most people will not live in a house without adequate heat. You need to be very careful before you criticize.

Distribution Problems

Most of the comfort complaints people have with home heating systems have more to do with uneven or inadequate distribution than inadequate capacity.

A New Home Example

A new 1,600–square foot home that is reasonably well insulated and weather-tight may require about 25 BTU per square foot. On its design day, it would need 40,000 BTU. If the boiler had a steady-state efficiency of 80 percent, it would have to have an input capacity of 50,000 BTU per hour.

Example in an Older Home

If you look at an older 1,600–square foot home that is not well insulated, you may need 50 BTU per square foot to keep it warm.

This means that on its design day it would lose 80,000 BTU per hour and we need a boiler with steady-state output of 80,000 BTU per hour. Assuming a steady-state efficiency of 80 percent, the boiler would have an input capacity of 100,000 BTU per hour.

These are common residential boiler sizes. Most home inspectors very quickly develop a sense of whether a boiler is adequate, even without doing a rough calculation. Since there are so many variables, you have to be a little careful, but you do want to raise the issue, at least where the system seems clearly undersized.

What Our Standards Require

Our standards don't require us to comment on the adequacy of heating to various areas. You don't need to go into any great detail on this, but a homeowner will have a hard time understanding why you failed to tell them their heating system couldn't possibly heat the house. A court might also have difficulty understanding that.

7.3   SEQUENCE OF OPERATION OF CONVENTIONAL BOILERS

From among the several possible operation sequences, we'll talk about a few of the more common ones in these two scenarios:

1. A system where the water in the boiler is kept hot all winter

2. A system where the boiler is allowed to cool when there is no demand for heat

7.3.1   Boiler Water Kept Hot All Winter

Starting Point

The house is comfortable. There is no call for heat. The water in the boiler is kept anywhere between 100°F and 200°F. The burner comes on and off as necessary to keep the water in the boiler at this temperature. A primary control (operating control) is used to keep the boiler heated within the desired range.

Pump Is off

The circulator is at rest. A flow control valve is normally used to prevent convection flow of the heated water through the system, since this might overheat the house.

When the house cools—

■ the thermostat calls for heat
■ the circulator is activated

- hot water flows through the pipes to the radiators
- the rooms are heated by the hot radiators
- the boiler sees cold water when the circulating pump comes on
- the water temperature drops below the cut-in setting on the primary control
- the burner is activated
- the thermostat is satisfied
- the circulator shuts off
- the burner keeps firing until the water in the boiler reaches the cutout temperature of the primary control
- the burner shuts off
- the burner cycles on and off as needed to keep the water hot

7.3.2   The Boiler Cools When the System Is at Rest

We'll look at three different possibilities.

The Circulator Runs Continuously

Starting Point

In this system, the circulator runs continuously throughout the heating season. There is no flow control valve.

When the system is at rest, the water in the boiler is cool (perhaps as low as room temperature) and the burner is off.

1. The thermostat calls for heat.
2. The burner comes on.
3. The water in the boiler is heated.
4. The circulator carries the hot water through the pipes to the radiators.
5. The radiators heat the rooms.
6. The thermostat is satisfied.
7. The burner turns off.
8. The water cools.
9. The pump continues to run.

The Circulator Is on While the Burner Is on

This system is typical with copper-tube boilers, for example. These boilers can't afford to have the burner on when the circulator is not. These boilers do not typically have a flow control valve.

Starting Point

When the system is at rest, the water is cool (perhaps at room temperature), the circulator pump is off, and the burner is off.

1. The thermostat calls for heat.
2. The burner and pump both come on.
3. Water in the boiler heats up.
4. The heated water is carried through the pipes to the radiators.
5. The radiators heat the rooms.
6. The thermostat is satisfied.

7. The burner turns off and the pump turns off (note: sometimes the pump runs for a couple of minutes after the burner shuts off).

8. The water in the boiler cools.

The Circulator Comes on at a Set Temperature

In this system, there is typically no flow control valve. At rest, the water is cool, the pump is off, and the burner is off.

1. The thermostat calls for heat.

2. The burner comes on.

3. The water in the boiler heats up.

4. When the water in the boiler hits the cut-in temperature for the pump (eg, 110°F), the circulator comes on.

5. Hot water is carried through the pipes and radiators.

6. The radiators heat the rooms.

7. The thermostat is satisfied.

8. The burner shuts off.

9. The pump runs until the temperature drops below the pump cut-in temperature (eg, 110°F).

10. The pump stops.

11. The water in the boiler cools.

Many Variations

As we discussed, there are many variations. Zoned systems can have different operating sequences. Large systems and some radiant systems don't use room thermostats to control the heat. These use outdoor temperature sensors to adjust the temperature of the water circulating through the system. On these systems, the boiler water may always be kept hot. A water blender may be used to mix cold water in with the hot water to deliver a predetermined temperature of water through the distribution system.

Regional Differences

We've talked about a number of systems already. In any given region of North America, usually only some of these are popular. Speak to local service people and heating contractors to find out which operating systems you're most likely to see. There's not much point in becoming expert at something you won't see regularly.

7.4 SEQUENCE OF OPERATION – MID-OR HIGH-EFFICIENCY BOILER WITH FORCED-DRAFT FAN

1. Make sure there is water in the boiler! Never fire up a dry boiler. Check the pressure gauge on the boiler, or open a bleed valve

2. The system is at rest, in standby mode.

3. Thermostat calls for heat.

4. Pump comes on.

5. Fan comes on for a 15-second pre-purge.

6. Air pressure switches prove the airflow.

7. Ignition system "on" (some igniters have to heat up for 15 to 30 seconds).

8. Gas valves open.

  9. Flame is verified within 5 seconds, typically.
10. Igniter shuts down.
11. Burner continues to operate.
12. Hot water is distributed through pipes and radiators.
13. Rooms are heated.
14. Thermostat is satisfied.
15. Burner shuts down.
16. Pump shuts down.
17. Fan stays on for 30 seconds post-purge.
18. Fan shuts off.
19. System enters standby mode.

CHAPTER REVIEW QUESTIONS

Answer the following questions on a separate sheet of paper, then check your results against the answers provided in Appendix E. If you have trouble with a question, refer back to the chapter to review the relevant material.

1. Describe the sequence of operation for a system where the boiler cools when the system is at rest. Assume that the circulating pump runs continuously.

2. What is the average lifespan of a cast-iron boiler?

KEY TERM

life expectancy

A P P E N D I X

STANDARDS OF PRACTICE

A.1 THE ASHI STANDARDS OF PRACTICE

The following are excerpted from the ASHI Standards of Practice effective, January 1, 2000.

8.0 Heating System

8.1 The *inspector* shall:
A. *Inspect:*

1. the *installed* heating equipment.

2. the vent systems, flues, and chimneys.

B. *describe:*

1. the energy source.

2. the heating method by its distinguishing characteristics.

8.2 The *inspector* is not required to:
A. *inspect:*

1. the interiors or flues or chimneys which are not *readily accessible*.

2. the heat exchanger.

3. the humidifier or dehumidifier.

4. the electronic air filter.

5. the solar space heating *system*.

B. determine heat supply adequacy or distribution balance.

12. General Limitations and Exclusions

12.1 General limitations:
A. Inspections performed in accordance with these standards of practice

1. are not *technically exhaustive*.

2. will not identify concealed conditions or latent defects.

B. These standards of practice are applicable to buildings with four or fewer dwelling units and their garages or carports.

12.2 General exclusions:

A. The inspector is not required to perform any action or make any determination unless specifically stated in these standards of practice, except as may be required by lawful authority.

B. Inspectors are NOT required to determine:

1. the condition of *systems* or *components* which are not *readily accessible.*

2. the remaining life of any *system* or *component.*

3. the strength, adequacy, effectiveness, or efficiency of any *system* or *component.*

4. the causes of any condition or deficiency.

5. the methods, materials, or costs of corrections.

6. future conditions including, but not limited to, failure of *systems* and *components.*

7. the suitability of the property for any specialized use.

8. compliance with regulatory requirements (codes, regulations, laws, rdinances, etc.).

9. the market value of the property or its marketability.

10. the advisability of the purchase of the property.

11. the presence of potentially hazardous plants or animals including, but not limited to wood destroying organisms or diseases harmful to humans.

12. the presence of any environmental hazards including, but not limited to toxins, carcinogens, noise, and contaminants in soil, water and air.

13. the effectiveness of any *system* installed or methods utilized to control or remove suspected hazardous substances.

14. the operating costs of *systems* or *components.*

15. the acoustical properties of any *system* or *component.*

C. *Inspectors* are NOT required to offer:

1. or perform any act or service contrary to law.

2. or perform *engineering* services.

3. or perform work in any trade or any professional service other than *home inspection.*

4. warranties or guarantees of any kind.

D. *Inspectors* are NOT required to operate:

1. any *system* or *component* which is *shut down* or otherwise inoperable.

2. any *system* or *component* which does not respond to *normal operating controls.*

3. shut-off valves.

E. *Inspectors* are NOT required to enter:

1. any area which will, in the opinion of the *inspector,* likely be dangerous to the inspector or other persons or damage the property or its *systems* or *components.*

2. The under-floor crawl spaces or attics which are not readily accessible.

F. *Inspectors* are NOT required to *inspect:*

1. underground items including, but not limited to underground storage tanks or other underground indications of their presence, whether abandoned or active.

2. *systems* or *components* which are not *installed.*

3. *decorative* items

4. *systems* or *components* located in areas that are not entered in accordance with these standards of practice.

5. detached structures other than garages and carports.

6. common elements or common areas in multi-unit housing, such as condominium properties or cooperative housing.

G. *Inspectors* are NOT required to:

1. perform any procedure or operation which will, in the opinion of the *inspector,* likely be dangerous to the inspector or other persons or damage the property or its *systems* or *components.*

2. move suspended ceiling tiles, personal property, furniture, equipment, plants, soil, snow, ice, or debris.

3. *dismantle* any *system* or *component,* except as explicitly required by these standards of practice.

NOTES ON THE STANDARDS

Accessible

We have to inspect house components that are readily accessible. That means we don't have to move furniture, lift carpets or ceiling tiles, dismantle components, damage things or do something dangerous. The exception is covers that would normally be removed by homeowners during routine maintenance. The furnace fan cover is a good example because homeowners remove this to change the furnace filter. Many inspectors use tools as the threshold. If tools are required to open or dismantle the component, it is considered not readily accessible.

Installed

We only have to inspect things that are installed in homes. This means we don't have to inspect window air conditioners or portable heaters, for example.

Deficiencies

We have to report on systems that are significantly deficient. This means they are unsafe or not performing their intended function.

End of Life

We are required to report on any system or component that in our professional opinion is near the end of its service life. This is tricky since we don't know whether inspectors will be held accountable for failed components on the basis that we should have known the component was near the end of its life. With the wisdom of hindsight, it may be hard to argue that the component could not have been expected to fail, when in fact, it did. Time will tell. The situation is also tricky because it includes not only systems but individual components as well. For many systems there are broadly accepted life expectancy ranges, but these aren't available for some individual components.

Remaining Life

We are not required to determine the remaining life of systems or components. This is related to, but different than, the end of service life issue. If the item is new or in the middle part of its life, we don't have to predict service life, even though the same broadly accepted life expectancy ranges would apply. It's only when the item is near the end, in your opinion, that you have to report it.

Reporting Implications

We have to tell people in writing the implications of conditions or problems unless they are self-evident. A cracked heat exchanger on a furnace has a very different implication for a homeowner than a cracked windowpane, for example.

Tell Client What To Do

We have to tell the client in the report what to do about any conditions we found. We might recommend they repair, replace, service or clean the component. We might advise them to have a specialist further investigate the condition. It's all right to tell the client to monitor a situation, but you can't tell them that their roof shingles are curled and leave it at that.

What We Left out

We have to report anything that we would usually inspect but didn't. We also have to include in our report why we didn't inspect it. The reasons may be that the component was inaccessible, unsafe to inspect or was shut down. It may also be that the occupant or the client asked you not to inspect it.

Installed

The standards say we have to inspect **installed** heating systems. This means we don't have to inspect portable heaters.

Controls

The standards say that we have to use **normal operating controls** to *inspect* heating systems. This means the thermostat. However, you don't have to operate the **automatic safety controls.** If you test the pressure-relief valve on a boiler, you may have trouble getting it closed. If you test a furnace on a high-temperature limit, you may start a fire by igniting the dust in the duct system. Unless you have specific training, do not operate automatic safety controls.

Heat Source in Each Room

We look for an installed heat source in each room, although the standards no longer ask for this specifically. If you find a room that does not have a heat source, this may be perfectly acceptable. For example, it may be a centrally located room with no exterior exposure at the walls, floor or ceiling.

Energy Source

We have to *describe* the energy source. That means we report whether the heating system fuel is gas, oil or electricity, for example.

Heating Method

We have to *describe* the heating method by its distinguishing characteristics. This means we have to say whether it is a furnace or a boiler. Further, we have to say whether thedistribution system is gravity warm air, forced air, gravity hot water, forced hot water, steam, or radiant heating, for example.

Open Panels

We have to open any panels that are there for homeowner inspection and maintenance. This means that we take the covers off conventional furnaces and open doors or remove access panels on boilers. The yardstick to use is whether the homeowner is expected to take these panels off to change filters, light pilots, etc. The panels have to be within normal reach, removable by one person, and not sealed in place.

Systems Shut down

We have to operate the system using the normal operating controls. Generally this means turning the thermostat up. If the system is shut down, you should note it in your report and explain why you could not test the heating system. We are not expected to light pilots or to start fires in wood stoves.

Sometimes We Don't Operate Systems

We don't have to operate the heating system when the weather conditions or something else might damage the heating system. For example, if the temperature is 90°F outside, you shouldn't test a heat pump in the heating mode. When it's 90°F outside, most people won't test a cast-iron radiator system on a hot water boiler to the point of making sure that each of the radiators gets warm. Starting a boiler up and getting heat to all the radiators takes some time. More importantly, it takes a good bit of time for a system like this to cool down. On a hot summer day, homeowners will be very unhappy that you have overheated their house. You'll have to use some common sense. Most inspectors test a system like this in hot weather only by making sure the boiler responds and the water starts to get warm. Good inspectors write this limited inspection issue in their reports.

Heat Exchanger

We do not have to *inspect* the **heat exchanger,** which is the heart of a furnace or boiler. The heat exchanger is at least partially concealed from view. Many home inspectors use mirrors and flashings to look at some of the heat exchanger, but most of it will not be seen. There are other methods of inspecting heat exchangers but these go beyond the standards. The standards release you from any responsibility for the heat exchanger.

Chimneys and Flues

We do have to *inspect* chimneys and their flues as well as their vents. However, we're not required to inspect the interior of chimneys or flues if they are not *readily accessible.* Most are not. Most inspectors look from the top and bottom where possible, but you can't be conclusive about the overall condition.

Uniformity/Adequacy of Heat

We do not have to inspect for the uniformity or adequacy of heat supply to the various rooms. On a hot summer day, this is virtually impossible to do, anyway. On a cold winter day, you won't have to do any testing; you'll notice as you walk through the house whether some rooms are cooler than others.

No Heat Loss Calculations

Home inspectors do not do heat loss calculations, they do not test high-temperature limits or pressure safety devices, and they do not dismantle heating systems.

Fuel Systems?

The Heating section of the standards is silent on checking fuel storage and distribution systems. However, in the Plumbing section, we have to observe fuel storage and distribution systems.

However, since this only applies to the plumbing system (for domestic water heating equipment) and not the heating system, you may be able to defend not checking the fuel system for the heating components at all. We check the fuel systems for heating and plumbing systems to be consistent, provide good service and avoid callbacks.

INSPECTION TOOLS

1. Flashlight

A good light is needed to look at the boiler, the fuel system and the venting system. You need to look at the outside and the inside of the boiler. The brighter the light, the better. Some inspectors use trouble lights (incandescent lights on cords) to inspect boilers.

2. Telescopic mirror

Mirrors are needed to look at heat exchangers, vents, draft hoods, etc.

Some inspectors carry a 1-inch by 1-inch mirror and a 2-inch by 3-inch mirror. Some heat exchangers are hard to get at.

3. Screwdrivers and pliers

While you shouldn't have to use tools to remove most covers, these tools are sometimes helpful to "persuade" stiff covers. Don't get carried away.

You should not dismantle the boiler, nor should you be making repairs.

For those who go beyond the standards and remove heat shields, you'll need a screwdriver for many of these.

4. Eyes, ears, nose and sense of touch

- As always, your eyes are your most important tool.

- Your ears will help you find bad bearings on motors, pumps, or fans, delayed ignition, etc.

- Gas, propane and oil all have distinctive smells. Your nose can help you find leaks. Your nose can help you detect spillage of exhaust products, too.

- Your sense of touch is used to detect overheating, exhaust gas spillage, loose components, etc.

5. Rags or towels

Boilers are usually dirty. You should carry something to clean your hands when you are finished inspecting the boiler. Some carry "wet wipes." Most inspectors avoid using the washroom in the house for clean up.

As you go through the rest of the house, you can't leave sooty fingerprints on everything you touch.

6. Car keys

These aren't necessary, but are used by many inspectors to remind them to turn the thermostat back down after testing. If you put your car keys on the thermostat when you turn the boiler up for testing, you can't leave the house until you retrieve your keys.

APPENDIX

C

✓ INSPECTION CHECKLIST

Location Legend
N = North, S = South, E = East, W= West, 1 = 1st story roof, 2 = 2nd story roof, 3 = 3rd story roof

Boilers

Location	**Gas Meters**
_____	❏ Rusting
_____	❏ Mechanical damage
_____	❏ Gas shut off and locked
_____	❏ Ice
_____	❏ Undersized
_____	❏ Poor access
_____	❏ Leaks
_____	❏ Poor location

Gas Piping
- _____ ❏ Leaks
- _____ ❏ Inappropriate materials
- _____ ❏ Inadequate support
- _____ ❏ Rusting
- _____ ❏ No drip leg
- _____ ❏ Missing shut off valves
- _____ ❏ Improper connections
- _____ ❏ Plastic pipe exposed above grade
- _____ ❏ Piping in chimney or duct systems
- _____ ❏ Copper tubing not properly labeled

Combustion Air
- _____ ❏ Inadequate combustion air

Gas Burner
- _____ ❏ Inoperative
- _____ ❏ Scorching
- _____ ❏ Poor flame color or pattern
- _____ ❏ Rust
- _____ ❏ Dirt or soot
- _____ ❏ Delayed ignition
- _____ ❏ Gas odor or leak
- _____ ❏ Short cycling

Heat Shield
- _____ ❏ Loose
- _____ ❏ Rusted
- _____ ❏ Missing
- _____ ❏ Scorched

Heat Exchangers
- _____ ❏ Leaks
- _____ ❏ Rust
- _____ ❏ Clogged

Location **Cabinets**
- _____ ❏ Rust
- _____ ❏ Mechanical damage
- _____ ❏ Missing components
- _____ ❏ Combustible clearance
- _____ ❏ Obstructed air intake
- _____ ❏ Scorching

Venting Systems
- _____ ❏ Rust
- _____ ❏ Poor slope
- _____ ❏ Vent connector too long
- _____ ❏ Poor support
- _____ ❏ Poor connections
- _____ ❏ Poor connections
- _____ ❏ Inadequate combustible clearance
- _____ ❏ Vent connector too big/too small
- _____ ❏ Improper material
- _____ ❏ Poor manifolding
- _____ ❏ Connector extends too far in chimney
- _____ ❏ Draft hood spillage
- _____ ❏ Vent connector dirty

Pressure Relief
- _____ ❏ Missing
- _____ ❏ Wrong size
- _____ ❏ Set wrong
- _____ ❏ Poor location
- _____ ❏ No piped extension
- _____ ❏ Pipe too small
- _____ ❏ Pipe threaded, capped or corroded at the bottom
- _____ ❏ Pipe dripping or leaking

High Temperature Limit Switch
- _____ ❏ Missing
- _____ ❏ Set too high
- _____ ❏ Defective/not wired correctly

Low Water Cutout
- _____ ❏ Leaking
- _____ ❏ Inoperative

Boilers

Location	**Backflow Preventer**
_____	❏ Missing
_____	❏ Leaking
_____	❏ Installed backwards

Pressure Reducing Valve
- _____ ❏ Set too low
- _____ ❏ Missing
- _____ ❏ Inoperative
- _____ ❏ Leaking
- _____ ❏ Installed backwards

Air Vent
- _____ ❏ Missing
- _____ ❏ Inoperative, clogged
- _____ ❏ Leaking

Primary Control
- _____ ❏ Inoperative
- _____ ❏ Set incorrectly

Pump Control
- _____ ❏ Inoperative
- _____ ❏ Set incorrectly

Zone Control
- _____ ❏ Inoperative
- _____ ❏ Leaking
- _____ ❏ Rust

Outdoor Air Thermostat
- _____ ❏ Inoperative

Flow Control Valve
- _____ ❏ Leaks
- _____ ❏ Inoperative
- _____ ❏ Rust

Isolating Valves
- _____ ❏ Leaks
- _____ ❏ Inoperative
- _____ ❏ Rust

Thermostats
- _____ ❏ Poor location
- _____ ❏ Not level
- _____ ❏ Loose
- _____ ❏ Dirty
- _____ ❏ Damaged
- _____ ❏ Poor adjustment/calibration
- _____ ❏ Anticipator problems

Location   Expansion Tank
- _____ ❏ Leaks
- _____ ❏ Waterlogged
- _____ ❏ Rust
- _____ ❏ Too small
- _____ ❏ Poor discharge location for open tank
- _____ ❏ Poor location for tank

Location   Circulator
- _____ ❏ Leaks
- _____ ❏ Inoperative
- _____ ❏ Noisy
- _____ ❏ Hot

Distribution Pipes
- _____ ❏ Rust
- _____ ❏ Leaks
- _____ ❏ Crimped
- _____ ❏ Too small
- _____ ❏ Poor support
- _____ ❏ No insulation

Radiators, Convectors and Baseboards
- _____ ❏ Leaks
- _____ ❏ Rust
- _____ ❏ Too small or too few
- _____ ❏ Missing
- _____ ❏ Poor location
- _____ ❏ Balancing valve problems
- _____ ❏ Bleed valve problems
- _____ ❏ Damaged baseboard fins
- _____ ❏ Obstructed air flow
- _____ ❏ Won't warm up

Radiant Heating
- _____ ❏ Leaks
- _____ ❏ Cool rooms or parts of rooms
- _____ ❏ Balancing valve problems
- _____ ❏ Bleed valve problems

Tankless Coils
- _____ ❏ Leaks
- _____ ❏ Rust
- _____ ❏ Clogged
- _____ ❏ Mixing valve missing
- _____ ❏ Set wrong
- _____ ❏ Defective

Mid- and High-Efficiency Boilers (Additional Conditions)
- _____ ❏ Cabinet problems
- _____ ❏ Fuel supply and burner problems
- _____ ❏ Combustion air and venting problems
- _____ ❏ Ignition problems
- _____ ❏ Heat exchanger problems
- _____ ❏ Safety and operating control problems
- _____ ❏ Induced-draft and forced-draft fan problems
- _____ ❏ Condensate handling problems

INSPECTION PROCEDURE

Inspecting heating systems is complicated. You will see many parts and many different systems.

We'll use strategies that include—

1. looking at the big picture, then looking at the individual components
2. looking for specific components and conditions, then looking at things to let them tell us their story

Checklists

On a heating system inspection, a checklist may be helpful. As you become more familiar with systems, you probably won't use a checklist on heating systems you see regularly. However, where you come across something that is unusual, you may want to rely on a checklist.

Not Exclusively

Again, we'll emphasize that you shouldn't rely exclusively on a checklist in any situation. Use the checklist to identify specific components and conditions to look for, but always take that step back and look at the big picture. What is the equipment trying to tell you?

The First Step

The first step in a heating system inspection is to identify the equipment:

1. Is it a furnace or a boiler?
2. What is the fuel?
   - Gas
   - Propane
   - Oil
   - Electricity
3. What is the distribution method?
   - Ducts and registers
   - Pipes and radiators or baseboards
   - Radiant piping
   - Electric radiant
4. How is combustion air supplied?
5. How are the exhaust products vented—through a chimney or through a side wall vent?

6. What safety controls should be in place? Can you find them?

7. What operating controls do you expect to find? Are they there?

8. What is the efficiency of the system—conventional, mid-efficiency or high-efficiency? You should expect different components and controls depending on the efficiency.

Look for Problems with Each Component

Once you have identified what you are dealing with, look for specific problems applicable to each. Many inspectors break the boiler inspection down into components. One way to break it down is as follows:

1. Fuel storage and delivery system

2. Combustion air

3. Burners

4. Heat exchangers

5. Cabinets

6. Controls

7. Venting systems

8. Distribution system

There is no magic to this approach. You can look at systems in whatever way works for you.

Fuel System

You can check the fuel system and combustion air without touching the boiler. Do this first, then get to the boiler.

Turn Power off

It is a good practice to turn the power off to the boiler before removing cover panels and looking inside. While you are doing it, you can also show your client how to turn the boiler on and off.

Remove the Cover

On many boilers, there is just one cover designed to be removed without tools. This is the cover for the burner compartment. (Just like everything else, there are exceptions.)

Once the cover is removed, you can get a closer look. Use your mirror and flashlight to look at the heat exchanger and other components that are difficult to see.

Many Problems

A checklist may help you find the many problems that may be on each component. As you are getting started, you will have to move slowly and take time to think things through as you look at each boiler. With experience, you will identify things more quickly and be able to move faster through this part of the inspection. However, it is not a race.

Turn Thermostat up

Turn the power back on and either turn up the thermostat, or have someone do it for you. It is helpful to have someone do it for you because then you can watch the startup sequence. Watching the burner start up is the only way you'll pick up things like delayed ignition, flashback on startup, etc.

Check Burner and Venting

Watch the burner as the system comes up to steady state. You should check the venting system for spillage or backdrafting, as well.

Close the Boiler Room Doors

When you are testing the boiler, make sure the room is set up the way it will normally be arranged. Don't leave the boiler room door open to give you more light. This will set up an artificial combustion air-supply situation. The burner may work fine with the boiler door open, and may be starved for air when the room is closed.

Watch the Sequence of Events

On a conventional boiler, expect the burner to come on, and then the circulator a couple of minutes later, as the water in the boiler heats up. Alternatively, the circulator may be energized when the burner is fired. There are other possibilities, as discussed in the text.

High Efficiency

On a high-efficiency condensing boiler, you'll be looking for other things. When the thermostat calls for heat, the induced- or forced-draft blower should come on for a few seconds before the igniter tries to light the burner. You'll have to know what kind of system you are looking at and how it should operate, before you can evaluate it.

Piping Leaks

Once the boiler is operating at steady state, you can check the performance of the distribution system. Where pipes are exposed, look for leakage.

Heat Supply

Check every room for an operable heating supply. Most inspectors just run their hand over radiators on hydronic systems to feel for heat delivery. You can get more sophisticated, but that goes beyond a home inspection.

Specific Boiler Walk-Through

Some inspectors leave the boiler running and do their inspection of the interior of the home, checking the heating supply system in each room as they go.

We suggest a separate walk-through of the house looking just at the heating performance. This helps you focus on the heating system and not be distracted by other components. It also allows you to cycle the boiler through and turn the temperature back to a normal setting without overheating the house.

Don't Leave the Thermostat Turned up

Doing a separate walk-through to check the heating system also helps to remind you to turn the thermostat down and put the burner cover back on the boiler. Since you'll be doing the rest of the inspection after this boiler check, you are more likely to stumble across it left on, or notice the house overheating if you have forgotten to turn the thermostat down.

Leave Keys on Thermostat

Many inspectors put their car keys on the thermostat when they turn the boiler up. This ensures they cannot leave the house until the thermostat is turned down.

Put Burner Cover on Your Tools

Many inspectors also put the burner cover on top of their tools or briefcase, so they can't possibly leave the house without stumbling across the cover. Others put the burner cover in a doorway or somewhere awkward to get around it. This has the disadvantage of other people perhaps tripping on the cover.

Put Things back

When you have finished, return the thermostat to its original setting. Replace the burner cover.

SUMMARY

Heating inspections are complex and demanding. You should establish a procedure that you repeat every time. Do not let yourself be distracted while checking the boiler. At the end of your inspection, double check to make sure that you have put everything back as you found it. Nothing makes a homeowner angrier than a house that has no heat or is too hot when they come home after you have been there.

APPENDIX E

ANSWERS TO CHAPTER REVIEW QUESTIONS

CHAPTER 1

1. Conduction is used to transfer heat from the products of combustion through the metal heat exchanger to the water.

2. b

3. c

4. ■ They provide very even heat.
   ■ They do not create drafts.
   ■ They are quieter than forced air furnaces.
   ■ They do not circulate odors.
   ■ The piping requires less room than ducts.
   ■ Boilers are smaller than furnaces for the same heat capacity.

5. ■ They are more costly to install and service.
   ■ It is more difficult to add central air, humidifying, and filtering equipment.
   ■ There is a greater selection of furnaces than boilers.
   ■ Radiators take up more space than heating registers.
   ■ A leak in a hot water system causes water damage.

6. Because the system is pressurized, the water can be heated beyond 212°F without creating steam. If this water is ever released, a steam explosion can result.

7. True

8. Adding fresh water each fall adds new oxygen to the system. This causes corrosion through the entire system.

CHAPTER 2

1. ■ Pressure relief valve;   ■ Low-water cutout;
   ■ High temperature limit;   ■ Backflow preventer

2. d

3. c

4. The pressure relief valve is located on top of the boiler, and typically discharges near the floor.

5. No

6. Yes

7. c

8. The low-water cutout prevents boiler damage if the system loses its water for any reason. The cutout prevents the boiler from firing.

9. To prevent contaminated boiler water from flowing backwards into the domestic water piping (drinking water) if the domestic side loses pressure for any reason.

10. b

11.
- Thermostat;
- Pressure reducing valve;
- Primary control;
- Pump control;
- Zone valves;
- Outdoor air thermostat

12. The pressure reducing valve drops the domestic water pressure (e.g., 60 psi.) down to the pressure required in the hydronic system (e.g., 15 psi.).

13. No

14. Yes

15. Automatic air vents get rid of air in the boiler water. They are not mandatory.

16. c

17. The pump can be controlled by water temperature, by the burner control including the thermostat, or be wired to run continuously when there is electrical power to the boiler.

18. Zone control allows different areas to receive different amount of heat to minimize cost, or maximize comfort. There are typically multiple thermostats in homes with zone control.

CHAPTER 3

1. Pump, piping, radiators, convectors or baseboards, and expansion tank

2. The open system operates at atmospheric pressure, the closed system is pressurized. The open system does not have a pump and does not need a pressure relief valve. An open system does not have automatic water make-up (pressure reducing valve).

3. Above the highest level radiator

4. The reverse return serves to make each piping loop similar length. This equalizes heat delivery to each room.

5. False

6. The expansion tank allows the water to expand as it is heated, so that excess pressure will not build up in the system.

7. Expansion tanks in closed systems are typically located near the boiler, often hung from the ceiling.

8. Pump and motor are mechanically coupled with bearings that have to be oiled.

- Pump and motor are close-coupled with permanently lubricated bushings.
- Pump and motor are close-coupled with water lubrication.

9. Black steel, copper, cast iron, plastic

10. a

11. Distribute heated water to the rooms, transfer heat to the rooms and return the cooled water to the boiler to be reheated.

CHAPTER 4

1. Radiator, convector, or baseboard
2. True
3. c
4. This allows the homeowner to remove trapped air from the radiator, letting the radiator fill with water and heat the room effectively.
5. Because they are turned rarely, the valve packing dries out and shrinks. When the valve is disturbed, a leak occurs here.

CHAPTER 5

1. c
2. Turn off the boiler supply water valve and turn off the boiler electrical supply. Watch for a drop in pressure at the temperature/pressure gauge on the boiler, indicating leakage out of the piping into the slab.
3. Yes
4. The water in the tankless coil is heated by boiler water, rather than a flame.
5. A side arm heater is mounted outside the boiler. Its function is identical to a tankless coil.
6. c
7. To reduce the temperature of the domestic water below the boiler water temperature to prevent scalding

CHAPTER 6

1. Vent damper, or induced-draft fan, and spark ignition.
2. No chimney needed, lower fuel costs from increased efficiency, direct venting
3.
- High efficiency boilers are expensive.
- Condensation is corrosive.
- Complex systems lead to high maintenance costs and poor reliability.

- High efficiency boilers may not be a good match for old piping and radiator systems.
- The radiator temperatures may be too low.
- The return water temperature is usually too high to encourage condensation in the products of combustion.
- The small volume boilers may overheat if the water flow through them is not adequate. Short cycling can be a problem.

4.
- Cabinet problems;
- Fuel supply and burner problems;
- Combustion air and venting problems;
- Ignition problems;
- Heat exchanger problems;
- Safety and operating control problems;
- Induced- and forced-draft fan problems;
- Condensate handling problems;
- Distribution problems;
- Inadequate waterflow through boiler—unique to high efficiency boilers;
- Noise—unique to high efficiency boilers (and high efficiency furnaces)

5. A combination system uses the domestic water heater to heat both the domestic water and living space. A tankless coil uses the boiler from a hydronic heating system to heat the domestic water.

CHAPTER 7

1.
- The thermostat calls for heat.
- The burner comes on.
- The water in the boiler is heated.
- The pump pushes the water through the piping to the radiators.
- The radiators heat the room.
- The thermostat is satisfied.
- The burner turns off.
- The water cools.
- The pump continues to run.

2. 35 to 50 years

INDEX